P9-COP-419

A Basket of
Gems

Compiled by Mark Stibbe and J. John:

A Box of Delights

A Barrel of Fun

A Bundle of Laughs

A Bucket of Surprises

Compiled by Mark Stibbe:

A Stocking Full of Christmas

The Bells! The Bells!

Compiled by Alie Stibbe and Killy John:

Bursting at the Seams

Compiled by Alie Stibbe:

All Stitched Up

Losing the Thread

A Basket of Gems

Compiled by

Mark Stibbe

MONARCH
BOOKS

Oxford, UK, & Grand Rapids, Michigan, USA

Copyright © 2009 by Mark Stibbe

The right of Mark Stibbe to be identified as author of this work
has been asserted by him in accordance with the
Copyright, Designs and Patents Act 1988.

All rights reserved. No part of this publication may be reproduced or
transmitted in any form or by any means, electronic or mechanical,
including photocopy, recording or any information storage and
retrieval system, without permission in writing from the publisher.

First published in the UK in 2009 by Monarch Books
(a publishing imprint of Lion Hudson plc),
Wilkinson House, Jordan Hill Road, Oxford OX2 8DR.
Tel: +44 (0)1865 302750 Fax: +44 (0)1865 302757
Email: monarch@lionhudson.com
www.lionhudson.com

ISBN: 978-1-85424-922-7 (UK)
ISBN: 978-0-8254-6319-8 (USA)

Distributed by:
UK: Marston Book Services Ltd, PO Box 269, Abingdon, Oxon OX14 4YN;
USA: Kregel Publications, PO Box 2607, Grand Rapids, Michigan 49501.

Illustrations by Darren Harvey-Regan

Unless otherwise stated, Scripture quotations are taken
from the Holy Bible, New International Version,
copyright © 1973, 1978, 1984 by the International Bible Society.
All rights reserved.

This book has been printed on
paper and board independently certified as
having come from sustainable forests.

British Library Cataloguing Data
A catalogue record for this book is available from
the British Library.

Printed and bound in Malta by Gutenberg Press.

Adventure

Adventure, with all its requisite danger and wilderness, is a deeply spiritual longing written into the soul of man.

John Eldredge

Age

The perks of being over fifty

If you are not over fifty, this is what you have to look forward to:

- Kidnappers are not very interested in you.
- In a hostage situation you are likely to be released first.
- No one expects you to run anywhere.
- People call at 9 p.m. and ask, 'Did I wake you?'
- People no longer view you as a hypochondriac.
- There is nothing left to learn the hard way.
- Things you buy now won't wear out.
- You can eat dinner at 4 p.m.
- You can live without sex but not without your glasses.
- You get into heated arguments about pension plans.
- You no longer think of speed limits as a challenge.
- You quit trying to hold your stomach in no matter who walks into the room.
- You sing along with elevator music.
- Your eyes won't get much worse.
- Your investment in health insurance is finally beginning to pay off.
- Your joints are more accurate meteorologists than the national weather service.
- Your secrets are safe with your friends because they can't remember them either.
- Your supply of brain cells is finally down to manageable size.
- You can't remember who sent you this list.

Exercise for people over fifty

Begin by standing on a comfortable surface, where you have plenty of room at each side. With a 5lb potato sack in each hand, extend your arms straight out from your sides and hold them there as long as you can. Try to reach a full minute, and then relax. Each day you'll find that you can hold this position for just a bit longer. After a couple of weeks, move up to 10lb potato sacks. Then try 50lb potato sacks and then eventually try to get to where you can lift a 100lb potato sack in each hand and hold your arms straight for more than a full minute. After you feel confident at that level, put a potato in each of the sacks.

Three ages of man

When you have the time and the energy, you don't have the money. When you have the money and the energy, you don't have the time. When you have the money and the time, you don't have the energy.

Ancestry

The following was overheard at a recent 'high society' party:

'My ancestry goes back all the way to Alexander the Great,' said Christine.

She then turned to Miriam and asked, 'How far back does your family go?'

'I don't know,' replied Miriam. 'All our records were lost in the flood.'

Anger

Husband: 'When I get mad at you, you never fight back. How do you control your anger?'

Wife: 'I clean the toilet bowl.'

Husband: 'How does that help?'

Wife: 'I use your toothbrush!'

There once was a little boy who had a bad temper. His father gave him a bag of nails and told him that every time he lost his temper, he must hammer a nail into the back of the fence. The first day the boy drove thirty-seven nails into the fence. Over the next few weeks, as he learned to control his anger, the number of nails hammered daily gradually dwindled down. He discovered it was easier to hold his temper than to drive those nails into the fence.

Finally the day came when the boy didn't lose his temper at all. He told his father about it and the father suggested that the boy now pull out one nail for each day that he was able to hold his temper. The days passed and the boy was finally able to tell his father that all the nails were gone.

The father took his son by the hand and led him to the fence. He said, 'You have done well, my son, but look at the holes in the fence. The fence will never be the same.'

When you say things in anger, they leave a scar just like this one. You can put a knife in a man and draw it out. It won't matter how many times you say you're sorry – the wound is still there. A verbal wound is as bad as a physical one.

Friends are very rare jewels indeed. They make you smile and encourage you to succeed. They lend an ear, they share words of praise and they always want to open their hearts to us.

Please forgive me if I have ever left a hole.

Apathy

A German man who lived in Nazi Germany told of his experience:

'I lived in Germany during the Nazi Holocaust. I considered myself a Christian. We heard stories of what was happening to the Jews, but we tried to distance ourselves from it, because, what could anyone do to stop it?

'A railroad track ran behind our small church, and each Sunday morning we could hear the whistle in the distance and then the wheels coming over the tracks. We became disturbed when we heard the cries coming from the train as it passed by. We realized that it was carrying Jews like cattle in the cars.

'Week after week the whistle would blow. We dreaded to hear the sound of those wheels because we knew that we would hear the cries of the Jews en route to the death camp. Their screams tormented us.

'We knew the time the train came past our church and when we heard the whistle blow we began singing hymns. By the time the train came past our church we were singing at the top of our voices. If we heard the screams, we sang more loudly and soon we heard them no more.

'Years have passed but I still hear that train whistle in my sleep. God forgive me; forgive all of us who called ourselves Christians and yet did nothing...'

Appearances

Regardless of the total size of an iceberg, approximately one ninth of it will be above the water.

A cool young man goes out and buys the best car available – a brand new Ferrari GTO. It is also the most expensive car in the world, and it costs him $550,000. He takes it out for a spin and stops for a red light. An old man on a moped, looking about 100 years old, pulls up next to him.

The old man looks at the sleek, shiny car and asks, 'What kind of car ya' got there, sonny?'

The young man replies, 'A Ferrari GTO. It cost half a million dollars!'

'That's a lot of money,' says the old man. 'Why does it cost so much?'

'Because this car can do up to 320 mph,' states the young dude proudly.

The moped driver asks, 'Mind if I take a look inside?'

'Not a problem,' replies the owner.

So, the old man pokes his head in the window and looks around. Then, sitting back on his moped, the old man says, 'That's a pretty nice car, all right – but I'll stick with my moped!'

Just then the light changes, so the guy decides to show the old man just what his car can do. He floors it, and within 30 seconds, the speedometer reads 160 mph!

Suddenly, he notices a dot in his rear-view mirror. It seems to be getting closer!

He slows down to see what it could be, and suddenly, *Whhhhhoooooooossssssshhh!* Something whips by him, going much faster!

'What on earth could be going faster than my Ferrari?' the young man asks himself. He floors the accelerator and takes the Ferrari up to 250 mph.

Then, up ahead of him, he sees that it is the old man on the moped! Amazed that the moped could pass his Ferrari, he gives it more gas and passes the moped at 275 mph.

He's feeling pretty good until he looks in his mirror and sees the old man gaining on him again. Astounded by the speed of this old guy, he floors the gas pedal and takes the Ferrari all the way up to 320 mph.

Not ten seconds later, he sees the moped bearing down on him again! The Ferrari is flat out, and there's nothing he can do! Suddenly, the moped ploughs into the back of his Ferrari, demolishing the rear end.

The young man stops and jumps out. He runs up to the mangled old man and says, 'Oh, my word! is there anything I can do for you?'

The old man whispers with his dying breath, 'Can you unhook my braces from your side-view mirror?'

Art

A thief in Paris planned to steal some paintings from the Louvre. After careful planning, he stole the paintings, got past security, and made it safely to his van.

However, he was captured only two blocks away when his van ran out of gas. When asked how he could mastermind such a crime and then make such an obvious error, he replied:

'Monsieur, that is the reason I stole the paintings. I had no Monet to buy Degas to make the Van Gogh.'

Assertiveness

A man went on an assertiveness course at work, and as a result decided that things needed to change at home, too.

When he got home he told his wife: 'I want supper on the table each evening when I get home from work. I want you to run me a hot bath and scrub my back. Then I want you to turn back the sheets, warm the bed and lay out my pyjamas. And in the morning, do you know who's going to button my shirt and tie my tie?'

'Yes,' replied his wife. 'The undertaker.'

Atheism

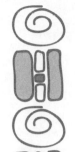

One day a six-year-old girl was sitting in a classroom. The teacher was going to explain evolution to the children. The teacher asked a little boy: 'Tommy, do you see the tree outside?'

Tommy: 'Yes.'

Teacher: 'Tommy, do you see the grass outside?'

Tommy: 'Yes.'

Teacher: 'Go outside and look up and see if you can see the sky.'

Tommy: 'OK.' He returned a few minutes later. 'Yes, I saw the sky.'

Teacher: 'Did you see God?'

Tommy: 'No.'

Teacher: 'That's my point. We can't see God because he isn't there. He just doesn't exist.'

A little girl spoke up and wanted to ask the boy some questions. The teacher agreed and the little girl asked the boy: 'Tommy, do you see the tree outside?'

Tommy: 'Yes.'

Little girl: 'Tommy, do you see the grass outside?'

Tommy: 'Yes!'

Little girl: 'Did you see the sky?'

Tommy: 'Yes!'

Little girl: 'Tommy, do you see the teacher?'

Tommy: 'Yes.'

Little girl: 'Do you see her brain?'

Tommy: 'No.'

Little girl: 'Then, according to what we were taught today in school, she can't have one!'

Baldness

I love bald men. Just because you've lost your fuzz, don't mean you ain't a peach.

Dolly Parton

Banks

The sub-prime crisis in Japan

Following the problems in the sub-prime lending market in America and the run on Northern Rock in the UK, uncertainty has now hit Japan.

In the last seven days Origami Bank has folded, Sumo Bank has gone belly up and Bonsai Bank has announced plans to cut some of its branches.

Yesterday it was announced that Karaoke Bank is up for sale and will likely go for a song, while today shares in Kamikaze Bank were suspended after they nose-dived.

While Samurai Bank are soldiering on following sharp cutbacks, Ninja Bank are reported to have taken a hit, but they remain in the black.

Furthermore, 500 staff at Karate Bank got the chop and analysts report that there is something fishy going on at Sushi Bank where it is feared that staff may get a raw deal.

Beatitudes

The Beatitudes as we would have written them

Happy are the 'pushers': for they get on in the world.

Happy are the hard-boiled: for they never let life hurt them.

Happy are they who complain: for they get their own way in the end.

Happy are the blasé: for they never worry over their sins.

Happy are the slave-drivers: for they get results.

Happy are the knowledgeable men of the world: for they know their way around.

Happy are the troublemakers: for they make people take notice of them.

J. B. Phillips

If the devil were to write his beatitudes, they would probably go something like this:

Blessed are those who seek worldly pleasures instead of seeking the will of God – they are my missionaries.

Blessed are the troublemakers – they shall be called my children.

Blessed are those who murmur and complain and have no joy – they really make my work easy.

Blessed are those who are focused on the minister's mannerisms and mistakes – for they get nothing out of his sermons.

Blessed are those who gossip – for they shall cause strife and divisions that please me.

Blessed are those who are easily offended – for they will soon get angry and quit.

Blessed is he who professes to love God but hates his brother and sister – for he shall be with me forever.

The lesson

Then Jesus took his disciples up the mountain and, gathering them around him, he taught them, saying:

Blessed are the poor in spirit, for theirs is the kingdom of heaven.

Blessed are the meek...

Blessed are they who mourn...

Blessed are the merciful...

Blessed are they who thirst for justice...

Blessed are you when persecuted...

Blessed are you when you suffer...

Be glad and rejoice, for your reward is great in heaven...

Then Simon Peter said, 'Do we have to write this down?'

And Andrew said, 'Are we supposed to know this?'

And James said, 'Will we have a test on it?'

And Philip said, 'What if we don't know it?'

And Bartholomew said, 'Do we have to turn this in?'

And John said, 'The other disciples didn't have to learn this.'

And Matthew said, 'When do we get out of here?'

And Judas said, 'What does this have to do with real life?'

Then one of the Pharisees present asked to see Jesus' lesson plans and asked him about his terminal objectives in the cognitive domain.

And Jesus wept...

Beginnings

If you plan to build a tall house of virtues,
you must first lay deep foundations of humility.
St Augustine

All difficult things have their origin in that which is easy,
and great things in that which is small.
Lao-Tsu

*All great deeds and all great thoughts have a ridiculous beginning.
Great works are often born on a street corner
or in a restaurant's revolving door.*
Albert Camus

Do not despise the bottom rungs in the ascent to greatness.
Publilius Syrus

The greatest masterpieces were once only pigments on a palette.
Henry S. Hoskins

A journey of a thousand miles must begin with a single step.
Lao-Tsu

***The man who removes a mountain begins
by carrying away small stones.***
Chinese proverb

Small opportunities are often the beginning of great enterprises.
Demosthenes

Start by doing what's necessary; then do what's possible;
and suddenly you are doing the impossible.
St Francis of Assisi

Take the first step in faith.
You don't have to see the whole staircase, just take the first step.
Martin Luther King Jr

You don't have to be great to start, but you have to start to be great.
Joe Sabah

Belief

First thing every morning before you arise say out loud, 'I believe.'

Norman Vincent Peale

Bellringers

The bellringers of Notre Dame

After Quasimodo's death, the bishop of the Cathedral of Notre Dame sent word through the streets of Paris that a new bellringer was needed.

The bishop decided that he would conduct the interviews personally and went up into the belfry to begin the screening process. After observing several applicants demonstrate their skill, he had decided to call it a day. Just then, an armless man approached him and announced that he was there to apply for the bellringer's job.

The bishop was incredulous. 'You have no arms!'

'No matter,' said the man. 'Observe!'

And he began striking the bells with his face, producing a beautiful melody on the carillon. The bishop listened in astonishment, convinced he had finally found a replacement for Quasimodo.

But suddenly, rushing forward to strike a bell, the armless man tripped and plunged headlong out of the belfry window to his death in the street below. The stunned bishop rushed to his side. When he reached the street, a crowd had gathered around the fallen figure, drawn by the beautiful music they had heard only moments before.

As they silently parted to let the bishop through, one of them asked, 'Bishop, who was this man?'

'I don't know his name,' the bishop sadly replied, *'but his face rings a bell!'*

The following day, despite the sadness that weighed heavily on his heart due to the unfortunate death of the armless campanologist, the bishop continued his interviews for the bellringer of Notre Dame.

The first man to approach him said, 'Your Excellency, I am the brother of the poor armless wretch that fell to his death from this very belfry yesterday. I pray that you honour his life by allowing me to replace him in this duty.'

The bishop agreed to give the man an audition, and, as the armless man's brother stooped to pick up a mallet to strike the first bell, he groaned, clutched at his chest, twirled around, and died on the spot.

Two monks, hearing the bishop's cries of grief at this second tragedy, rushed up the stairs to his side. 'What has happened? Who is the man?' the first monk asked breathlessly.

'I don't know his name,' sighed the distraught bishop, 'but...' (wait for it...) 'he's a dead ringer for his brother.'

Bible

The mobile phone versus the Bible

What would happen if we treated our Bibles in the same way we treat our mobile phones?

What if we carried it around in our handbags or pockets?

What if we flipped through it several times a day?

What if we turned back to get it if we forgot it?

What if we used it to receive messages?

What if we treated it as though we could not live without it?

What if we gave it to our children as a gift?

What if we used it when we travelled?

What if we used it in emergencies?

We do not have to worry about our Bible being disconnected because of an unpaid bill. Jesus has already paid the bill, and in full.

And just think – no missed calls! God hears them all.

Anne Robinson: 'The Bible, the New Testament. The Four Gospels were written by Matthew, Mark, Luke and…?'

Contestant: *(long pause)* 'Joe?'

The Weakest Link, BBC TV programme

The story is told of an old man who lived on a farm in the mountains of eastern Kentucky with his young grandson. Each morning, Grandpa was up early, sitting at the kitchen table reading from his old worn-out Bible. His grandson, who wanted to be just like him, tried to imitate him in any way he could.

One day the grandson asked, 'Grandpa, I try to read the Bible just like you but I don't understand it, and what I do understand I forget as soon as I close the book. What good does reading the Bible do?'

The grandfather quietly turned from putting coal in the stove and said, 'Take this coal-basket down to the river and bring back a basket of water.'

The boy did as he was told, even though all the water leaked out before he could get back to the house.

The grandfather laughed and said, 'You will have to move a little faster next time,' and sent him back to the river with the basket to try again.

This time the boy ran faster, but again the basket was empty before he returned home. Out of breath, he told his grandfather that it was 'impossible to carry water in a basket', and he went to get a bucket instead.

The old man said, 'I don't want a bucket of water; I want a basket of water. You can do this. You're just not trying hard enough,' and he went out the door to watch the boy try again.

At this point, the boy knew it was impossible, but he wanted to show his grandfather that even if he ran as fast as he could, the water would leak out before he got very far. The boy scooped the water and ran hard, but when he reached his grandfather the basket was again empty.

Out of breath, he said, 'See, Grandpa, it's useless!'

'So you think it's useless?' The old man said, 'Look at the basket.'

The boy looked at the basket and for the first time he realized that it looked different. Instead of a dirty old coal-basket, it was clean.

'Son, that's what happens when you read the Bible. You might not understand or remember everything, but when you read it, it will change you from the inside out. That is the work of God in our lives – to change us from the inside out and to slowly transform us into the image of his Son.'

Birthdays

'Hello, this is the police. How may I help you?'

'I'm calling to report my neighbour, Mark. He's hiding drugs inside his firewood.'

'Thank you very much for the call, sir.'

The next day, the drug officers descended on Mark's house. They searched the shed where the firewood was kept. Using axes, they busted open every piece of wood, but found no drugs. They swore at Mark, he swore at them, and then they left.

The next day, the phone rang at Mark's house.

'Hey, Mark! Did the police come to your house?'

'Yeah.'

'Did they chop your firewood?'

'Yep.'

'Happy birthday, buddy!'

Bossiness

A large company, feeling it was time for a shake-up, hired a new CEO. The new boss was determined to rid the company of all slackers. On a tour of the facilities, the CEO noticed a guy leaning on a wall. The room was full of workers and he wanted to let them know that he meant business.

He walked up to the guy leaning against the wall and asked, 'How much money do you make a week?'

A little surprised, the young man looked at him and replied, 'I make $400 a week. Why?'

The CEO then handed the guy $1,600 in cash and screamed, 'Here's four weeks' pay. Now *get out* and don't come back!'

Feeling pretty good about himself, the CEO looked around the room and asked, 'Does anyone want to tell me what that goofball did here?'

From across the room came a voice: 'He's the pizza delivery guy from Domino's.'

Boys

Christian boys' chat–up lines

'Nice Bible.'

'Is this pew taken?'

'I just don't feel called to celibacy.'

'For you I would slay two Goliaths.'

'I would go through more than the Book of Job for you.'

'Shall we tithe?'

'At points in my life I have been referred to as Samson.'

'The Bible says, "Give drink to those who are thirsty, and feed the hungry." So how about dinner?'

'I didn't believe in predestination until tonight.'

'I believe one of my ribs belongs to you.'

Bulletins

These sentences (with all the 'bloopers') actually appeared in church bulletins or were announced in church services:

- The Fasting & Prayer will include meals.
- Next Thursday there will be try-outs for the choir. They need all the help they can get.
- The Scouts are saving aluminium cans, bottles and other items to be recycled. Proceeds will be used to cripple children.
- Please place your donation in the envelope along with the deceased Person you want remembered.
- The church will host an evening of fine dining, super entertainment and gracious hostility.

- This evening at 7 p.m. there will be a hymn singing in the park across from the church. Bring a blanket and come prepared to sin.
- Ladies' Bible Study will be held Thursday morning at 10 a.m. All ladies are invited to lunch in the Fellowship Hall after the B.S. is done.
- The eighth-graders will be presenting Shakespeare's *Hamlet* in the church basement Friday at 7 p.m. The congregation is invited to attend this tragedy.
- Weight Watchers will meet at 7 p.m. at the First Presbyterian Church. Please use the large double door at the side entrance.

Call

Answering the call of our Creator is 'the ultimate why' for living, the highest source of purpose in human existence. Apart from such a calling, all hope of discovering a purpose will end in disappointment... Nothing short of God's call can ground and fulfil the truest human desire for purpose.

Os Guinness, The Call: Finding and Fulfilling the Central Purpose of Your Life
(Thomas Nelson, 2003)

Cannibals

Q. What did the cannibal say when he came upon a sleeping missionary?

A. 'Ah! Breakfast in bed!'

Cats

According to a study presented in February 2008 to the conference of the American Stroke Association, cat ownership has a positive effect on heart health. Those with cats who participated in the study showed a 30 per cent reduction in the risk of heart attack, even after taking into account important biological risk factors.

Characters

Most likely, at least once a day you delete a letter, number, or even whole words and paragraphs from your documents on the computer. It's a simple matter for you, but have you ever thought about the consequences of your action? Do you have any idea where you're sending those characters that you so casually rejected? The answer varies, depending on whom you ask.

Dave Barry's explanation: 'The deleted characters are shipped to Battle Creek, Michigan, where they're made into Pop-Tart filling; this explains why Pop-Tarts are so flammable, while cheap imitations are not as flammable.'

Stephen King's explanation: 'Every time you hit the delete key you unleash a tiny monster inside the cursor, who tears the poor unsuspecting characters to shreds, drinks their blood, then eats them, bones and all.'

IBM's explanation: 'The characters are not real. They exist only on the screen when they are needed, as concepts, so to delete them is merely to de-conceptualize them.'

The Buddhist explanation: 'If a character has lived rightly, and its karma is good, then after it has been deleted it will be reincarnated as a different, higher character. Those funny characters above the numbers on your keyboard will become numbers, numbers will become letters, lower-case letters will become upper case. If a character's karma is not so good, then it will move down the above scale, ultimately becoming the lowest of characters – a space.'

The twenty-first-century bitter, cynical nihilist explanation: 'Who cares? All characters are the same, swirling in a vast sea of meaningless nothingness. It doesn't really matter if they're on the page, deleted, undeleted, underlined, etc. It's all the same. More characters should delete themselves.'

The environmentalist's explanation: 'You've been *deleting* them? Can't you hear them *screaming*? Little innocent characters and baby lower-case letters have rights too!'

Children

The way children see things

NUDITY

I was driving with my three young children one warm summer evening when the woman in the convertible ahead of us stood up and waved. She was stark naked! As I was reeling from the shock, I heard my five-year-old shout from the back seat, 'Mum! That lady isn't wearing a seat belt!'

HONESTY

My son Zachary, age four, came screaming out of the bathroom to tell me he'd dropped his toothbrush in the toilet. So I fished it out and threw it in the garbage. Zachary stood there thinking for a moment, then ran to the bathroom and came out with my toothbrush. He held it up and said with a charming little smile, 'We'd better throw this one out too then, 'cause it fell in the toilet a few days ago.'

OPINIONS

On the first day of school, a first-grader handed his teacher a note from his mother. The note read, 'The opinions expressed by this child are not necessarily those of his parents.'

KETCHUP

A woman was trying hard to get the ketchup to come out of the bottle.

I'm not sure I can cope taking another register with those four kids in the class

STAFF

During her struggle the phone rang, so she asked her four-year-old daughter to answer the phone. 'It's the minister, Mummy,' the child said to her mother. Then she added, 'Mummy can't come to the phone to talk to you right now. She's hitting the bottle.'

MORE NUDITY

A little boy got lost at the YMCA and found himself in the women's locker room. When he was spotted, the room burst into shrieks, with ladies grabbing towels and running for cover. The little boy watched in amazement and then asked, 'What's the matter? Haven't you ever seen a little boy before?'

THE ELDERLY

While working for an organization that delivers lunches to elderly shut-ins, I used to take my four-year-old daughter on my afternoon rounds. The various appliances of old age, particularly the canes, walkers and wheelchairs, unfailingly intrigued her. One day I found her staring at a pair of false teeth soaking in a glass. As I braced myself for the inevitable barrage of questions, she merely turned and whispered, 'The tooth fairy will never believe this!'

DRESS-UP

A little girl was watching her parents dress for a party. When she saw her dad donning his tuxedo, she warned, 'Daddy, you shouldn't wear that suit.'

'And why not, darling?'

'You know that it always gives you a headache the next morning.'

DEATH

While walking along the pavement in front of his church, our minister heard the intoning of a prayer that nearly made his collar wilt. Apparently, his five-year-old son and his playmates had found a dead robin. Feeling that a proper burial should be performed, they had found a small box, then dug a hole and made ready for the disposal of the deceased. The minister's son was chosen to say the appropriate prayers and with sonorous dignity intoned his version of what he thought his father always said: 'Glory be unto the Faaaather, and unto the Sonnn ... and into the hole he gooooes.'

SCHOOL

A little girl had just finished her first week of school. 'I'm just wasting my time,' she said to her mother. 'I can't read, I can't write and they won't let me talk!'

THE BIBLE

A little boy opened the big family Bible. He was fascinated as he fingered through the old pages. Suddenly, something fell out of the Bible. He picked up the object and looked at it. What he saw was an old leaf that had been pressed in between the pages.

'Mum, look what I found!' the boy called out.

'What have you got there, dear?'

With astonishment in his voice, he answered, 'I think it's Adam's underwear!'

Choices

We live today in a world in which nobody believes choices should have consequences. But may I tell you the great secret that our culture seeks to deny? You cannot escape the consequences of your choices. Time runs in only one direction.

The character Jack Ziegler in The Emperor of Ocean Park
by Stephen L. Clark

Church

The Church used to be a *lifeboat*... now it's a *cruise ship*. We're not marching to Zion, we're sailing there with ease... In the Apostolic church it says they were all amazed and now in all our churches everybody wants to be amused. The Church began in the upper room despised, in the upper room with a bunch of men agonizing and it's ended up in the supper room with a bunch of women organizing. We mistake rattle for revival and commotion for creation and action for unction.

Leonard Ravenhill

This is God's ultimate achievement
– a community; a centre of
warm, pulsating, effervescent,
outreaching Christian love; a place
with all its components united in
order to become a force in this
world rather than a farce.
Dr Gilbert Bilezikian

Going to church doesn't make you a Christian any more than going to McDonalds makes you a hamburger.

Keith Green

Q. What do an aeroplane, a bicycle and a church have in common?
A. If any of them stop moving forward, you're in trouble!

Circumcision

Back in the time when samurai were important, there was a powerful emperor who needed a new chief samurai, so he sent a declaration throughout the land that he was searching for the very best.

A year passed, and only three people showed up for the trials: a Japanese samurai, a Chinese samurai and a Jewish samurai.

The emperor asked the Japanese samurai to come in and demonstrate why he should be Chief samurai. The Japanese samurai opened a matchbox, and out flew a bumble-bee. *Whoosh!* went his razor-sharp sword, and the bumble-bee dropped dead on the ground in two pieces.

The emperor exclaimed: 'This is most impressive!'

The emperor then issued the same challenge to the Chinese samurai – to come in and demonstrate why he should be chosen. The Chinese samurai also open a matchbox, and out buzzed a fly. *Whoosh, whoosh!* went his great flashing sword, and the fly dropped dead on the ground… in four small pieces.

The emperor exclaimed in awe: 'That is really *very* impressive!'

Now the emperor turned to the Jewish samurai, and asked him also to step forward and demonstrate why he should be the Head samurai. The Jewish samurai also opened a matchbox, and out flew a small gnat. His lightning-quick sword went *Whoosh! Whoosh! Whoosh!* But the gnat was still alive and flying around.

The emperor was obviously very disappointed by this display, and said: 'I see you are not up to the task. The gnat is not dead.'

The Jewish samurai just smiled and said, 'Circumcision is not meant to kill.'

Citizenship

We are not citizens of this world trying to make our way to heaven; we are citizens of heaven trying to make our way through this world.

Coincidences

- Abraham Lincoln was elected to Congress in 1846.
- John F. Kennedy was elected to Congress in 1946.
- Abraham Lincoln was elected President in 1860.
- John F. Kennedy was elected President in 1960.
- Both were particularly concerned with civil rights.
- Both wives lost their children while living in the White House.
- Both Presidents were shot on a Friday.
- Both Presidents were shot in the head.
- Now it gets really weird. Lincoln's secretary was named Kennedy.
- Kennedy's secretary was named Lincoln.
- Both were assassinated by Southerners.
- Both were succeeded by Southerners named Johnson.
- Andrew Johnson, who succeeded Lincoln, was born in 1808.
- Lyndon Johnson, who succeeded Kennedy, was born in 1908.
- John Wilkes Booth, who assassinated Lincoln, was born in 1839.
- Lee Harvey Oswald, who assassinated Kennedy, was born in 1939.
- Both assassins were known by their three names.
- Both names are composed of fifteen letters.
- Now hang onto your seat. Lincoln was shot at the theatre named Ford.
- Kennedy was shot in a car called a Lincoln made by Ford.
- Lincoln was shot in a theatre and his assassin ran and hid in a warehouse.
- Kennedy was shot from a warehouse and his assassin ran and hid in a theatre.
- Booth and Oswald were assassinated before their trials.
- And here's the kicker. A week before Lincoln was shot, he was in Monroe, Maryland.
- A week before Kennedy was shot, he was with Marilyn Monroe.

Commitment

We are all saddened to learn this week of the death of one of our church's most valuable members, Someone Else. Someone's passing created a vacancy that will be difficult to fill. Else has been with us for many years, and for every one of those years, Someone did far more than a normal person's share of the work.

Whenever leadership was mentioned, this wonderful person was looked to for inspiration as well as results: 'Someone Else can work with that group.'

Whenever there was a job to do, a class to teach, or a meeting to attend, one name was on everyone's lips: Someone Else! 'Let Someone Else do it' was a common refrain heard throughout the church.

It was common knowledge that Someone Else was among the largest givers in the church. Whenever there was a financial need, everyone just assumed Someone Else would make up the difference.

Someone Else was a wonderful person, sometimes appearing superhuman; but a person can only do so much. Were the truth known, everybody expected too much of Someone Else.

Now Someone Else is gone! We wonder what we are going to do. Someone Else left a wonderful example to follow, but who is going to follow it? Who is going to do the things Someone Else did?

Remember – we can't depend on Someone Else any more!

This is a story of four people named Everybody, Somebody, Anybody and Nobody.

There was an important job to be done and Everybody was asked to do it. Everybody was sure that Somebody would do it. Anybody could have done it. But Nobody did it. Somebody got angry about that because it was Everybody's job.

Everybody thought Anybody could do it, but Nobody realized that Everybody wouldn't do it. It ended up that Everybody blamed Somebody, when Nobody did what Anybody could have done!

I am part of the fellowship of the unashamed. I have the Holy Spirit power. The die has been cast. I have stepped over the line. The decision has been made – I'm a disciple of His. I won't look back, let up, slow down, back away or be still. My past is redeemed, my present makes sense, my future is secure. I'm finished and done with low-living, sight-walking, colourless dreams, tamed visions, worldly talking, cheap giving, and dwarfed goals.

I no longer need pre-eminence, prosperity, position, promotions, plaudits or popularity. I don't have to be right, to be first, to be recognized, to be praised, to be regarded, or to be rewarded. I now live by faith, lean on his presence, walk by patience, am uplifted by prayer, and I labour with power.

My life is set, my goal is heaven, my road is narrow, my way is rough, my real companions are few, my guide is reliable, my mission is clear.

I cannot be bought, compromised, detoured, lured away, turned back, deluded or delayed. I will not flinch in the face of sacrifice, hesitate in the presence of the enemy, or wander in the maze of mediocrity. I won't give up, shut up, let up until I have stayed up, stored up, prayed up, paid up, preached up for the cause of Christ.

I am a disciple of Jesus. I must go till He comes, give till I drop, preach till all know and work till he stops me. And when He comes for His own, He will have no problem recognizing me.

My banner will be clear.

This inspiring statement by Dr Bob Moorehead has been widely admired and quoted. It was found in the desk drawer of a young Zimbabwean pastor who had been brutally executed.

Communication

There was this truck driver who had to deliver 500 penguins to the state zoo. As he was driving his truck through the desert, it broke down. After about three hours, he waved another truck down and offered the driver $500 to take the penguins to the state zoo for him.

The next day the first truck driver arrived in town and saw the other truck driver crossing the road with 500 penguins walking in single file behind him.

The first truck driver jumped out of his truck and asked, 'What's going on? I gave you $500 to take these penguins to the zoo!'

The other truck driver responded, 'I did take them to the zoo. And I had some money left over, so now we're going to see a movie.'

Community

Things that Christians should do

- *Love* one another: John 13:34; 15:12; 1 Thessalonians 3:12; 4:9; 1 Peter 1:22; 1 John 3:18.
- *Encourage* one another: 1 Thessalonians 4:18; Hebrews 10:24.
- *Spur* one another on (towards love and good deeds): Hebrews 10:24.
- *Build* one another up: 1 Thessalonians 5:11; Romans 14:19.
- *Admonish* one another: Colossians 3:16.
- *Instruct* one another: Romans 15:14.
- *Serve* one another: Galatians 5:13; 1 Peter 4:10.
- *Bear* with one another: Ephesians 4:32; Colossians 3:13.
- *Forgive* one another: Ephesians 4:32; Colossians 3:13.
- *Be kind* to one another: Ephesians 4:32.
- *Be compassionate* to one another: Ephesians 4:32; 1 Peter 3:8.
- *Be devoted* to one another: Romans 12:10.
- *Honour* one another: Romans 12:10.
- *Live in harmony* with one another: Romans 12:16; 1 Peter 3:8.
- *Be sympathetic* with one another: 1 Peter 3:8.
- *Be patient* with one another: Ephesians 4:2.
- *Accept* one another: Romans 15:7.
- *Submit* to one another: Ephesians 5:21.
- *Clothe yourselves with humility* towards one another: Ephesians 4:2; 1 Peter 5:5.
- *Teach* one another: Colossians 3:16.
- *Live at peace* with one another: Mark 9:50; Romans 12:18.
- *Confess* your sins to one another: James 5:16.
- *Offer hospitality* to one another: 1 Peter 5:14.
- *Greet one another*: Romans 16:16; 1 Peter 5:14.
- *Have fellowship* with one another: 1 John 1:7.
- *Agree* with one another: 1 Corinthians 1:10.
- *Carry* one with another: Galatians 6:2.

Prohibitions in Christian fellowship

- Do not *hurt/harm* one another: Galatians 5:15.
- Do not *irritate* one another: Galatians 5:26.
- Do not be *jealous* of one another: Galatians 5:26.
- Do not *hate* one another: Titus 3:3.
- Do not *judge* one another: Romans 14:13.
- Do not *lie* to one another: Colossians 3:9.
- Do not *criticize* one another: James 4:11.
- Do not *complain* against one another: James 5:9.
- Do not take *legal proceedings* against one another: 1 Corinthians 6:1–8.

It is easy to deceive yourself with beautiful thoughts of loving God. However you must prove your love for God by your love for your brother, that is the one standard by which God will judge your love for him. If the love of God is in your heart, you will undoubtedly love your brother.

Andrew Murray

Compassion

His name is Bill. He is a student. He has wild hair, wears a T-shirt with holes in it, jeans and no shoes. This was his wardrobe for his entire four years at college.

Across the street from his accommodation is a conservative, well-dressed church. They want to develop a ministry to the students but they don't know how to go about it.

One day Bill decides to visit the church. He walks in with no shoes, jeans, his T-shirt and wild hair. The service has already started and so Bill walks down the aisle looking for a seat. The church is completely packed and he can't find anywhere to sit. By now people are really looking a bit uncomfortable, but no one says a thing.

Bill gets closer and closer to the pulpit and, when he realizes there are no seats, he just squats down right on the carpet. By now the people are really uptight, and the tension in the air is thick.

About this time the minister realizes that from the back of the church one of the deacons is slowly making his way towards Bill. The deacon is in his eighties, has silver-grey hair, and a smart three-piece suit. A godly man, very elegant, very dignified, very courtly. He walks with a cane and, as he approaches Bill, everyone is thinking to themselves, 'You can't blame him for what he is about to do.'

It takes a long time for the old man to reach the boy. The church falls silent. Nothing can be heard save the tapping of the deacon's cane. All eyes are focused on him. The minister has paused before beginning his sermon. Everyone holds their breath.

And then they see something amazing. The deacon drops his cane on the floor and with great difficulty he lowers himself and sits down next to Bill so he won't be alone.

Everyone gasps. When the minister regains his poise, he says, 'What I'm about to preach, you will never remember. But what you have seen, you will never forget. Be careful how you live. You may be the only Bible some people read.'

Complaining

The letter below was actually sent to a bank by a client. The Bank Manager thought it amusing enough to have it published in the *New York Times*.

Dear Sir:

I am writing to thank you for bouncing my cheque with which I endeavoured to pay my plumber last month. By my calculations, three nanoseconds must have elapsed between his presenting the cheque and the arrival in my account of the funds needed to honour it. I refer, of course, to the automatic monthly deposit of my entire salary, an arrangement which, I admit, has been in place for only eight years.

You are to be commended for seizing that brief window of opportunity, and also for debiting my account $30 by way of penalty for the inconvenience caused to your bank. My thankfulness springs from the manner in which this incident has caused me to rethink my errant financial ways.

I noticed that whereas I personally attend to your telephone calls and letters, when I try to contact you, I am confronted by the impersonal, overcharging, pre-recorded, faceless entity that your bank has become.

From now on, I, like you, choose only to deal with a flesh-and-blood person. My mortgage and loan repayments will therefore and thereafter no longer be automatic, but will arrive at your bank, by cheque, addressed personally and confidentially to an employee at your bank whom you must nominate.

Be aware that it is an offence under the Postal Act for any other person to open such an envelope. Please find attached an Application Contact Status which I require your chosen employee to complete. I am sorry it runs to eight pages, but in order that I know as much about him or her as your bank knows about me, there is no alternative. Please note that all copies of his or her medical history must be counter-signed by a Notary Public, and the mandatory details of his/her financial situation (income, debts, assets and liabilities) must be accompanied by documented proof.

In due course, I will issue your employee with a PIN number which he/she must quote in dealings with me. I regret that it cannot be shorter than 28 digits but, again, I have modelled it on the number of button presses required of me to access my account balance on your phone bank service. As they say, imitation is the sincerest form of flattery.

Let me level the playing field even further. When you call me, press the buttons as follows:

1. To make an appointment to see me.
2. To query a missing payment.
3. To transfer the call to my living-room in case I am there.
4. To transfer the call to my bedroom in case I am sleeping.
5. To transfer the call to my toilet in case I am attending to nature.
6. To transfer the call to my mobile phone if I am not at home.
7. To leave a message on my computer, a password to access my computer is required. Password will be communicated to you at a later date to the Authorised Contact.
8. To return to the main menu and to listen to options 1 through to 7.
9. To make a general complaint or enquiry.

The contact will then be put on hold, pending the attention of my automated answering service. While this may, on occasion, involve a lengthy wait, uplifting music will play for the duration of the call.

Regrettably, but again following your example, I must also levy an establishment fee to cover the setting up of this new arrangement.

May I wish you a happy, if ever so slightly less prosperous New Year?

Your Humble Client…

Computers

A surgeon, a civil engineer and a software engineer were chatting. The discussion rolled around to whose profession was the oldest.

The surgeon said that his was, since in the Book of Genesis, God created Eve from one of Adam's ribs, and surely that involved surgery.

The civil engineer countered by saying that before God created man, he created the heavens and the earth from chaos – surely a feat of civil engineering.

The software engineer just smiled and said, 'Where do you think chaos came from?'

Classic computer helpline requests

When people were installing software and the instructions said, 'Hit any key to continue', the most common helpline problem was, 'I can't find any key.'

A woman rings up: 'My mouse does not work. I've put it on the floor beneath the computer and it does not respond to my foot pressing on it.'

A man rings up: 'My Internet Fax program does not work. I printed my letter, held it against the screen and clicked Send.'

Customer: 'My keyboard is not working any more.'

Tech Support: 'Are you sure it's plugged into the computer?'

Customer: 'No. I can't get behind the computer.'

Tech Support: 'Pick up your keyboard and walk ten paces back.'

Customer: 'OK.'

Tech Support: 'Did the keyboard come with you?'

Customer: 'Yes.'

Tech Support: 'That means the keyboard is not plugged in. Is there another keyboard?'

Customer: 'Yes, there's another one here. Ah… that one does work…'

Tech Support: 'Click on the "My Computer" icon on the left of the screen.

Customer: 'Your left or my left?'

Tech Support: 'What kind of computer do you have?'

Customer: 'A white one.'

Customer: 'Hi, this is Martha. I can't print. Every time I try, it says "Can't find printer". I've even lifted the printer and placed it in front of the monitor, but the computer still says he can't find it.'

Tech Support: 'How may I help you?'

Customer: 'I'm writing my first e-mail.'

Tech Support: 'OK, and what seems to be the problem?'

Customer: 'Well, I have the letter "a" in the address, but how do I get the circle around it?'

A woman customer called the Canon help desk about a problem with her printer.

Tech Support: 'Are you running it under Windows?'

Customer: 'No, my desk is next to the door, but that is a good point. The man sitting in the cubicle next to me is under a window, and his printer is working fine.'

Confession

A drunken man staggered into a Catholic church and sat down in a confession box, saying nothing.

The bewildered priest coughed to attract his attention, but still the man said nothing.

The priest then knocked on the wall three times in a final attempt to get the man to speak.

Finally, the drunk replied, 'No use knockin', mate. There's no paper in this one either.'

A parish priest was being honoured at a dinner on the twenty-fifth anniversary of his arrival in that parish. A leading local politician, who was a member of the congregation, was chosen to make the presentation and to give a little speech at the dinner. But he was delayed in traffic, so the priest decided to say his own few words while they waited.

'You will understand,' he said, 'the seal of the confessional can never be broken. However, I got my first impressions of the parish from the first confession I heard here. I can only hint vaguely about this, but when I came here twenty-five years ago I thought I had been assigned to a terrible place. The very first chap who entered my confessional told me how he had stolen a television set, and when stopped by the police, had almost murdered the officer! Further, he told me he had embezzled money from his place of business and had had an affair with his boss's wife. I was appalled! But as the days went on, I learned that my people were not all like that, and I had indeed come to a fine parish full of understanding and loving people.'

Just as the priest finished his talk, the politician arrived full of apologies at being late. He immediately began to make the presentation and give his talk.

'I'll never forget the first day our parish priest arrived in this parish,' said the politician. 'In fact, I had the honour of being the first one to go to him in confession.'

Conversion

Myra Hindley, one of the perpetrators of the infamous Moors Murders, was baptized a Catholic but not brought up as one.

She said, 'I wish I could put complete trust in God, but I am frightened to do so, for my faith is full of doubt and despair that I'll never be good enough to merit complete forgiveness.'

She wrote to Lord Longford: 'I don't think I could adequately express just how much it means to me to have been to Confession and to have received Holy Communion – it is a terrifying beautiful thing; terrifying because I have taken a step which has taken me on the threshold of a completely new way of life which demands so much more from me than my previous one, and beautiful because I feel spiritually re-born. I made such a mess of my old life and I thank God for this second chance...it doesn't matter whether I live in prison or outside.'

Quotations from the biography of Lord Longford

Cricket

The rules of cricket

You have two sides. One is out in the field and one is in.

Each man that's in the side that's in goes out, and when he is out he comes in, and the next man goes in until he is out.

When they are all out, the side that's out comes in and the side that's been in goes out and tries to get those coming in out.

Sometimes you may get men still in and not out.

When both sides have been in and out, including the not outs, that's the end of the game.

Howzat!

Criticism

If you judge people, you have no time to love them.

Mother Teresa

I'd rather be an artist than an art critic. I'd rather be a movie-maker than a movie critic. I'd rather be a musician than a music critic. And I'd rather be a church builder than a church critic.

A young lady named Sally relates an experience she had in a seminary class given by her teacher, Dr Smith. She says that Dr Smith was known for his elaborate object lessons. One particular day, Sally walked into the seminary and knew they were in for a fun day.

On the wall was a big target and on a nearby table were many darts. Dr Smith told the students to draw a picture of someone that they disliked or someone who had made them angry, and he would allow them to throw darts at the person's picture.

Sally's friend drew a picture of the woman who had stolen her boyfriend. Another friend drew a picture of his little brother. Sally drew a picture of a former friend, putting a great deal of detail into her drawing, even drawing pimples on the face. Sally was pleased with the overall effect she had achieved.

The class lined up and began throwing darts. Some of the students threw their darts with such force that their targets were ripping apart. Sally looked forward to her turn, and was filled with disappointment when Dr Smith, because of time limits, asked the students to return to their seats. As Sally sat thinking about how angry she was because she didn't have a chance to throw any darts at her target, Dr Smith began removing the target from the wall.

Underneath the target was a picture of Jesus. A hush fell over the room as each student viewed the mangled picture of Jesus. Holes and jagged marks covered his face and his eyes were pierced.

Dr Smith said only these words: 'In as much as ye have done it unto the least of these my brethren, ye have done it unto me' (Matthew 25:40).

Death

It was about 1850, March, snow flurries, frozen ground, a log cabin. And in that little log cabin on the prairie was a boy by the name of Timmy, who was dying of diphtheria. The pastor who came to that log cabin that day was a Methodist circuit rider; that is, he rode his horse hundreds of miles to cabins and churches, visiting them every two months or so. This pastor came into the cabin and inquired about Timmy, whom he had heard was sick. The pastor was ushered through an opening in the curtain to a back room where Timmy was sick in bed.

The pastor said, 'Timmy, do you know how to say the 23rd Psalm?'

'Yes, I learnt it when I was in second grade, in Sunday School. It goes like this. "The Lord is my shepherd. I shall not want…"' Timmy rattled off the 23rd Psalm rapidly.

'No, Timmy, that is not the way to say it.'

'OK, pastor, I will say it more slowly.'

'Timmy,' the pastor said, 'I want to teach you how to say the 23rd Psalm. As you begin the first sentence, you count your fingers, beginning with your thumb, and when you get to the fourth word, the word "my", you grab that finger. A wedding ring is on the fourth finger of your mother's and father's hands.

It is the finger of love. Say the words of the first sentence as you count your fingers, and then grab the fourth finger when you say the word "my". That will remind you that Jesus is always your personal shepherd, my personal shepherd. OK?'

So Timmy practised saying the first sentence of the Psalm. The pastor was satisfied. They said their goodbyes and the pastor left.

The pastor returned to the log cabin two months later and it was now spring. The snow was gone and as he approached the log cabin, he saw a little mound of dirt near the cabin with a cross on it. He knew Timmy had died.

The pastor went into the log cabin and talked with Timmy's parents. They talked about Timmy; they talked about his death; and finally the mother asked, 'You know, pastor, something strange happened when Timmy died. We kissed him goodnight. In the morning, first thing, we went behind the curtain to see him and he was gone; he had died. But it was so strange. His right hand was still wrapped around the fourth finger of his left hand. Do you know what that means, pastor?'

When you say the 23rd Psalm, you need to know how to say the first line: 'The Lord is…*my*…shepherd…'

On 11 April 1996 Larry LaPrise – the man who wrote 'The Hokey Kokey' – died peacefully, at the age of eighty-three. The most traumatic part for his family was getting him into the coffin. They put his left leg in... and then the trouble started.

Death is the one experience through which we all will pass. We may meet it with resignation, denial, or even without a moment's thought – but come it will.

But death for the believer is distinctly different from what it is for the unbeliever. For us, it isn't something to be feared or shunned, for we know death is but the shadowed threshold to the palace of God. No wonder Paul declared, 'I desire to depart and be with Christ, which is better by far' (Philippians 1:23, NIV).

Sometimes God gives His departing saints glimpses of Heaven (partly, I believe, to encourage those of us who remain). Just before dying my grandmother sat up in bed, smiled, and said, 'I see Jesus, and He has His hand outstretched to me. And there is Ben, and he has both of his eyes and both of his legs.' (Ben, my grandfather, had lost an eye and a leg at Gettysburg.)

Are you looking forward to that day when you will go to be with Christ, 'which is better by far'?

Billy Graham

Desire

I want deliberately to encourage this mighty longing after God. The lack of it has brought us to our present low estate. The stiff and wooden quality about our religious lives is a result of our lack of holy desire. Complacency is a deadly foe of all spiritual growth. Acute desire must be present or there will be no manifestation of Christ to His people. He waits to be wanted. Too bad that with many of us He waits so long, so very long, in vain.

A. W. Tozer

Disagreements

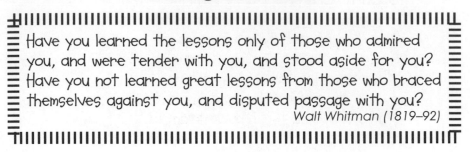

Have you learned the lessons only of those who admired you, and were tender with you, and stood aside for you? Have you not learned great lessons from those who braced themselves against you, and disputed passage with you?

Walt Whitman (1819–92)

Donkeys

A man bought a donkey from a preacher. The preacher told the man that this donkey had been trained in a very unique way (being the donkey of a preacher). The only way to make the donkey go was to say, 'Hallelujah!' The only way to make the donkey stop was to say, 'Amen!'

The man was pleased with his purchase and immediately got on the animal to try out the preacher's instructions.

'Hallelujah!' shouted the man. The donkey began to trot.

'Amen!' shouted the man. The donkey stopped immediately.

'This is great!' said the man. With a 'Hallelujah!' he rode off, very proud of his new purchase.

The man travelled for a long time through the mountains. As he headed towards a cliff, he tried to remember the word to make the donkey stop.

'Stop,' said the man. 'Halt!' he cried. The donkey just kept going.

'Oh no! Bible!... Church!... Please! Stop!!' shouted the man.

The donkey just began to trot faster. He was getting closer and closer to the edge of the cliff.

Finally, in desperation, the man said a prayer. 'Please, dear Lord. Please make this donkey stop before I go off the end of this mountain. *Amen!*'

The donkey came to an abrupt stop just one step from the edge of the cliff.

'*Hallelujah!*' shouted the man.

Dreams

Dreams are extremely important. You can't do it unless you imagine it.

George Lucas

Driving

Sitting on the side of a highway in the States, waiting to catch speeding drivers, a police officer sees a car puttering along at 22 mph. He thinks to himself, 'This driver is just as dangerous as a speeder!' So he turns on his lights and pulls the driver over.

Approaching the car, he notices that there are five old ladies – two in the front and three in the back – wide-eyed and white as ghosts. The driver, obviously confused, says to him, 'Officer, I don't understand, I was doing exactly the speed limit! What seems to be the problem?'

'Ma'am,' the officer replies, 'you weren't speeding, but you should know that driving slower than the speed limit can also be a danger to other drivers.'

'Slower than the speed limit? No sir, I was doing exactly 22 miles an hour!' the old woman says a bit proudly.

The officer, trying to contain a chuckle, explains to her that '22' is the highway number, not the speed limit.

A bit embarrassed, the woman grins and thanks the officer for pointing out her error.

'But before I let you go, ma'am, I have to ask, is everyone in this car OK? These women seem awfully shaken and they haven't muttered a single peep this whole time,' the officer says.

'Oh, they'll be all right in a minute, officer. We just got off Highway 119.'

When I die, I want to go like my grandmother, who died peacefully in her sleep. Not screaming, like all the passengers in her car.

While driving in Pennsylvania, a family caught up to an Amish carriage. The owner of the carriage obviously had a sense of humour, because attached to the back of the carriage was a hand-printed sign: 'Energy-efficient vehicle. Runs on oats and grass. Caution: do not step in exhaust.'

Dynamite

A fellow from Michigan buys himself a brand-new $30,000 Jeep Grand Cherokee for Christmas. He goes down to his favourite bar and celebrates by tossing down a few too many brews with his buddies. In one of those male bonding rituals, five of them decide to take his new vehicle for a test drive on a duck-hunting expedition. They load up the Jeep with the dog, the guns, the decoys, and the beer, and head out to a nearby lake.

Now, it's the dead of winter, and of course the lake is frozen, so they need to make a hole in the ice to create a natural landing area for the ducks and decoys. It is common practice in Michigan to drive your vehicle out onto the frozen lake, and it is also common (if slightly illegal) to make a hole in the ice using dynamite. Our fellows have nothing to worry about on that score, because one member of the party works for a construction team, and happens to have brought some dynamite along. The stick has a short twenty-second fuse.

The group is ready for some action. They're all set up. Their shotguns are loaded with duck pellets, and they have beer, warm clothes and a hunting dog. Still chugging down a seemingly bottomless supply of six-packs, the group considers how to safely dynamite a hole through the ice. One of these rocket scientists points out that the dynamite should explode at a location far from where they are standing. Another notes the risk of slipping on the ice when running away from a burning fuse.

So they eventually settle on a plan to light the fuse and throw the dynamite out onto the ice. There is a bit of contention over who has the best throwing arm, and eventually the owner of the Jeep wins that honour. Once that question is settled, he walks about twenty feet further out onto the ice and holds the stick of dynamite at the ready while one of his companions lights the fuse with a Zippo. As soon as he hears the fuse sizzle, he hurls it across the ice at a great velocity and runs in the other direction.

Unfortunately, a member of another species spots his master's arm motions and comes to an instinctive decision. Remember a couple of moments ago when I mentioned the vehicle, the beer, the guns and… the dog? Yes, the dog: a trained Black Labrador, born and bred for retrieving, especially things thrown by his owner. As soon as the stick leaves his hand, the dog sprints across the ice, hell-bent on wrapping his jaws around the enticing stick-shaped object.

Five frantic fellows immediately begin hollering at the dog, trying to get him to stop chasing the dynamite. Their cries fall on deaf ears. Before you know it, the retriever is headed back to his owner, proudly carrying the stick of dynamite with the burning twenty-second fuse.

The group continues to yell and wave their arms while the happy dog trots towards them. In a desperate act, its master grabs his shotgun and fires at his own dog. The gun is loaded with duck shot, and confuses the dog more than it hurts him. Bewildered, he continues towards his master, who shoots at man's best friend again.

Finally comprehending that his owner has become insane, the dog runs for cover with his tail between his legs. And the nearest cover is right under the brand-new Jeep Grand Cherokee.

Boom! The dog and the Jeep are blown to bits, and sink to the bottom of the lake, leaving a large ice hole in their wake.

The stranded men stand staring at the water with stupid looks on their faces, and the owner of the Jeep is left to explain the misadventure to his insurance company. Needless to say, they determine that sinking a vehicle in a lake by illegal use of explosives is not covered under their policy, and the owner is still making $400 monthly payments on his brand-new Jeep at the bottom of the lake.

Easter

Crosses are not the places where faith is killed but where it is proven.
Calvin Miller,
author of
The Christ of Easter

I owe my Lord a morning song, for Jesus rose at dawn; he made death die and would not lie, that others might live on.
John L. Bell

Each day, 5 million marshmallow chicks and bunnies are produced in preparation for Easter.
The National Confectioners' Association

The cross is the way of the lost
the cross is the staff of the lame
the cross is the guide of the blind
the cross is the strength of the weak
the cross is the hope of the hopeless
the cross is the freedom of the slaves
the cross is the water of the seeds
the cross is the consolation of the labourers
the cross is the source of those who seek water
the cross is the cloth of the naked
African hymn from
444 Surprising Quotes about Jesus

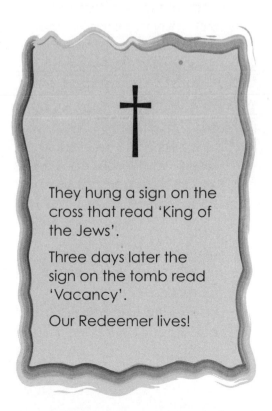

They hung a sign on the cross that read 'King of the Jews'.

Three days later the sign on the tomb read 'Vacancy'.

Our Redeemer lives!

Elvis

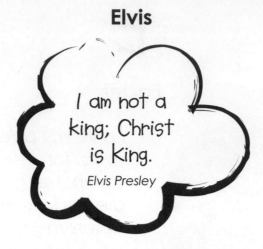

I am not a king; Christ is King.

Elvis Presley

Encouragement

Encouragement is such a great gift for leaders to dole out. All it takes is thought and time, yet the impact is lasting. As William Ward said, 'Flatter me, and I may not believe you. Criticize me, and I may not like you. Ignore me, and I may not forgive you. Encourage me, and I will not forget you.'

Here are some thoughts on how we as leaders can give the gift of encouragement to our co-workers not only at Christmas, but also throughout the year:

- Attune yourself to notice the positive.
- Be very liberal with praise.
- Compliment them frequently, sincerely, and publicly.
- Learn the names of their spouses, children and friends and use them.
- Note their hobbies and special interests and watch for articles that may be of interest to them.
- Work on your own self-image. You cannot love others if you do not like yourself. I find leaders who are not encouraging often need to focus on this.
- Give credit where credit is due.
- Ask, 'How can I help?'
- Give appropriate challenges. People get bored when they are not challenged.
- Listen! Really listen to them.

Dr Carson Pue

England

Once upon a time in the Kingdom of Heaven, God went missing for six days. Eventually, Michael the archangel found him on the seventh day resting. He enquired of God, 'Where have you been?'

God pointed downwards through the clouds. 'Look, Michael. Look what I've made!' said God.

Archangel Michael looked puzzled and said, 'What is it?'

'It's a planet,' replied God, 'and I've put *life* on it. I'm going to call it Earth and it's going to be a great place of balance.'

'Balance?' enquired Michael, still confused.

God explained, pointing down to different parts of the Earth, 'For example, North America will be a place of great opportunity and wealth while South America is going to be poor. The Middle East over there will be a hot-spot and Russia will be a cold spot. Over there I've placed a continent of white people and over there is a continent of black people.'

God continued, pointing to the different countries. 'This one will be extremely hot and arid while this one will be very cold and covered in ice.'

The Archangel, impressed by God's work, then pointed to another area of land and asked, 'What's that?'

'Ah,' said God. 'That's the North of England, the most glorious place on earth. There are beautiful people – look at the great cities in Lancashire alone – and many impressive towns. It is the home of the world's finest artists, musicians, writers, thinkers, explorers and politicians. The people from North England are going to be modest, intelligent and humorous and they're going to be found travelling the world. They'll be extremely sociable, hard-working and high-achieving, and they will be known throughout the world as speakers of truth.'

Michael gasped in wonder and admiration but then proclaimed, 'What about balance, God? You said there will be *balance*.'

God replied very wisely, 'Wait till you see the bunch of people I'm putting down South!'

Evangelism

When we seek out that which is lost, we are loving our neighbour as we love ourselves and valuing people as God values them. If we as the Church keep this as our core focus and mission, we will never become an empty building or mere tourist attraction. We will be so occupied and fulfilled with doing what the Church was placed on this earth to do – taking what is inside the Church out into a broken world – that our doors will never close. The lost will be drawn to us because of our open arms and our loving, safe environment.

Christina Caine, Stop Acting Like a Christian, Just Be One *(Regal, 2007)*

John Harper, the true hero of the *Titanic*

John Harper was born to a pair of solid Christian parents on May 29th, 1872. It was on the last Sunday of March 1886, when he was thirteen years old that he received Jesus as the Lord of his life. He never knew what it was to 'sow his wild oats.' He began to preach about four years later at the ripe old age of 17 years old by going down to the streets of his village and pouring out his soul in earnest entreaty for men to be reconciled to God.

As John Harper's life unfolded, one thing was apparent...he was consumed by the word of God. When asked by various ministers what his doctrine consisted of, he was known to reply 'The Word of God!' After five or six years of toiling on street corners preaching the gospel and working in the mill during the day, Harper was taken in by Rev. E. A. Carter of Baptist Pioneer Mission in London, England. This set Harper free to devote his whole time and energy to the work so dear to his heart. Soon, John Harper started his own church in September of 1896. (Now known

as the Harper Memorial Church.) This church which John Harper had started with just 25 members, had grown to over 500 members when he left 13 years later. During this time he had gotten married, but was shortly thereafter widowed. However brief the marriage, God did bless John Harper with a beautiful little girl named Nana.

Ironically, John Harper almost drowned several times during his life. When he was two and a half years of age, he almost drowned when he fell into a well but was resuscitated by his mother. At the age of twenty-six, he was swept out to sea by a reverse current and barely survived, and at thirty-two he faced death on a leaking ship in the Mediterranean. Perhaps, God used these experiences to prepare this servant for what he faced next...

It was the night of April 14, 1912. *The RMS Titanic* sailed swiftly on the bitterly cold ocean waters heading unknowingly into the pages of history. On board this luxurious ocean liner were many rich and famous people.

At the time of the ship's launch, it was the world's largest man-made moveable object. At 11:40 p.m. on that fateful night, an iceberg scraped the ship's starboard side, showering the decks with ice and ripping open six watertight compartments. The sea poured in.

On board the ship that night was John Harper and his much-beloved six-year-old daughter Nana. According to documented reports, as soon as it was apparent that the ship was going to sink, John Harper immediately took his daughter to a lifeboat. It is reasonable to assume that this widowed preacher could have easily gotten on board this boat to safety; however, it never seems to have crossed his mind. He bent down and kissed his precious little girl; looking into her eyes he told her that she would see him again someday. The flares going off in the dark sky above reflected the tears on his face as he turned and headed towards the crowd of desperate humanity on the sinking ocean liner.

As the rear of the huge ship began to lurch upwards, it was reported that Harper was seen making his way up the deck yelling, 'Women, children and unsaved into the lifeboats!' It was only minutes later that the Titanic began to rumble deep within. Most people thought it was an explosion; actually the gargantuan ship was literally breaking in half. At this point, many people jumped off the decks and into the icy, dark waters below. John Harper was one of these people.

That night 1,528 people went into the frigid waters. John Harper was seen swimming frantically to people in the water, leading them to Jesus before the hypothermia became fatal. Mr

Harper swam up to one young man who had climbed up on a piece of debris. Rev. Harper asked him between breaths, 'Are you saved?' The young man replied that he was not.

Harper then tried to lead him to Christ only to have the young man who was near shock, reply no. John Harper then took off his life jacket and threw it to the man and said, 'Here then, you need this more than I do...' and swam away to other people. A few minutes later Harper swam back to the young man and succeeded in leading him to salvation. Of the 1,528 people that went into the water that night, six were rescued by the lifeboats. One of them was this young man on the debris. Four years later, at a survivors' meeting, this young man stood up and in tears recounted how, after John Harper had led him to Christ, Mr Harper had tried to swim back to help other people, yet because of the intense cold, had grown too weak to swim. His last words before going under in the frigid waters were, 'Believe on the Name of the Lord Jesus and you will be saved.'

Does Hollywood remember this man? No. Oh well, no matter. This servant of God did what he had to do. While other people were trying to buy their way onto the lifeboats and selfishly trying to save their own lives, John Harper gave up his life so that others could be saved.

'Greater love hath no man than this, that he lay down his life for his friends.' John Harper was truly the hero of the *Titanic*!

Abridged from The Titanic's Last Hero *by Moody Adams (Moody Press, 1997)*

Evolution

■ ― ■ ― ■ ― ■ ― ■ ― ■ ― ■ ― ■ ― ■ ― ■ ― ■ ― ■ ― ■ ― ■

One day the zoo-keeper noticed that the monkey was reading two books –the Bible and Darwin's *The Origin of Species*. In surprise he asked the monkey, 'Why are you reading both those books?'

'Well,' said the monkey, 'I just wanted to know if I was my brother's keeper or my keeper's brother.'

■ ― ■ ― ■ ― ■ ― ■ ― ■ ― ■ ― ■ ― ■ ― ■ ― ■ ― ■ ― ■ ― ■

An open letter to the Kansas State Board of Education from Professor Philip S. Skell (Member, National Academy of Sciences; Evan Pugh Professor of Chemistry, Emeritus Penn State University):

May 12, 2005

Dr Steve E. Abrams, Chair
Kansas State Board of Education
c/o Kansas State Department of Education

Dear Dr Abrams

I have been following the controversy over the adoption of new science standards in your state with interest. I am writing – as a member of the National Academy of Sciences – to voice my strong support for the idea that students should be able to study scientific criticisms of the evidence for modern evolutionary theory along with the evidence favoring the theory.

All too often, the issue of how to teach evolutionary theory has been dominated by voices at the extremes. On one extreme, many religious activists have advocated for Bible-based ideas about creation to be taught and for evolution to be eliminated from the science curriculum entirely. On the other hand, many committed Darwinian biologists present students with an idealized version of the theory that glosses over real problems and prevents students from learning about genuine scientific criticisms of it.

Both these extremes are mistaken. Evolution is an important theory and students need to know about it. But scientific journals now document many scientific problems and criticisms of evolutionary theory and students need to know about these as well.

Many of the scientific criticisms of which I speak are well known by scientists in various disciplines, including the disciplines of chemistry and biochemistry, in which I have done my work. I have found that some of my scientific colleagues are very reluctant to acknowledge the existence of problems with evolutionary theory to the general public. They display an almost religious zeal for a strictly Darwinian view of biological origins.

Darwinian evolution is an interesting theory about the remote history of life. Nonetheless, it has little practical impact on those branches of science that do not address questions of biological history (largely based on stones, the fossil evidence). Modern biology is engaged in the examination of tissues from living organisms with new methods and instruments. None of the great discoveries in biology and medicine over the past century depended on guidance from Darwinian evolution – it provided no support.

As an aside, one might ask what Darwin would have written today if he was aware of the present state of knowledge of cell biology, rather than that of the mid 19th century when it was generally believed the cell was an enclosed blob of gelatin? As an exemplar, I draw your attention to what Prof. James A. Shapiro, bacteriologist, U. of Chicago, wrote (http://www.bostonreview.net/br22.1/shapiro.html).

For those scientists who take it seriously, Darwinian evolution has functioned more as a philosophical belief system than as a testable scientific hypothesis. This quasi-religious function of the theory is, I think, what lies behind many of the extreme statements that you have doubtless encountered from some scientists opposing any criticism of neo-Darwinism in the classroom. It is also why many scientists make public statements about the theory that they would not defend privately to other scientists like me.

In my judgment, this state of affairs has persisted mainly because too many scientists were afraid to challenge what had become a philosophical orthodoxy among their colleagues. Fortunately, that is changing as many scientists are now beginning to examine the evidence for neo-Darwinism more openly and critically in scientific journals.

Intellectual freedom is fundamental to the scientific method. Learning to think creatively, logically and critically is the most important training that young scientists can receive. Encouraging students to carefully examine the evidence for and against neo-Darwinism, therefore, will help prepare students not only to understand current scientific arguments, but also to do good scientific research.

I commend you for your efforts to ensure that students are more fully informed about current debates over neo-Darwinism in the scientific community.

Yours sincerely,
Professor Philip S. Skell

Exams

These are metaphors from actual GCSE essays:

- Her face was a perfect oval, like a circle that had its two other sides gently compressed by a Thigh Master.
- She caught your eye like one of those pointy hook latches that used to dangle from doors and would fly up whenever you banged the door open again.
- The little boat gently drifted across the pond exactly the way a bowling ball wouldn't.
- McMurphy fell twelve stories, hitting the pavement like a paper bag filled with vegetable soup.
- Her hair glistened in the rain like nose hair after a sneeze.
- Her eyes were like two brown circles with big black dots in the centre.
- He was as tall as a six-foot-three-inch tree.
- The politician was gone but unnoticed, like the full stop after the Dr. on a Dr Pepper can.
- John and Mary had never met. They were like two hummingbirds who had also never met.
- The thunder was ominous sounding, much like the sound of a thin sheet of metal being shaken backstage during the storm scene in a play.
- The red brick wall was the colour of a brick-red crayon.
- Even in his last years, Grandpa had a mind like a steel trap, only one that had been left out so long it had rusted shut.
- The door had been forced, as forced as the dialogue during the interview portion of *Family Fortunes*.
- Shots rang out, as shots are wont to do.
- 'Oh, Jason, take me!' she panted, her breasts heaving like a student on 31p-a-pint night.
- Her artistic sense was exquisitely refined, like someone who can tell butter from 'I Can't Believe It's Not Butter'.
- It came down the stairs looking very much like something no one had ever seen before.
- The knife was as sharp as the one used by Glenda Jackson MP in her first of several points of parliamentary procedure made to Robin Cook MP, Leader of the House of Commons, in the House Judiciary Committee hearings on the suspension of Keith Vaz MP.
- The ballerina rose gracefully *en pointe* and extended one slender leg behind her, like a dog at a lamp-post.

- The revelation that his marriage of thirty years had disintegrated because of his wife's infidelity came as a rude shock, like a surcharge at a formerly surcharge-free cash-point.
- The dandelion swayed in the gentle breeze like an oscillating electric fan set on 'Medium'.
- It was a working-class tradition, like fathers chasing kids around with their power tools.

- She walked into my office like a centipede with ninety-eight missing legs.
- Her voice had that tense, grating quality, like a first-generation thermal paper fax machine that needed a band tightened.

Excuses

A father had asked his son to paint a fence. When asked why he had failed to do it, the lad replied, 'Well, I would have, but I couldn't find the axe!'

'What's the axe got to do with it?' his father retorted.

'Nothing. But when you don't want to do something, one excuse is just as good as another!'

A senior citizen drove his brand-new BMW Z3 convertible out of the car salesroom. Taking off down the motorway, he floored it to 90 mph, enjoying the wind blowing through what little hair he had left.

'Amazing!' he thought as he flew down the M40, enjoying pushing the pedal to the metal even more. Looking in his rear-view mirror, he saw a police car behind him, blue lights flashing and siren blaring.

'I can get away from him – no problem!' thought the elderly nutcase as he floored it to 110 mph, then 120, then 130.

Suddenly, he thought, 'What on earth am I doing? I'm too old for this nonsense!' So he pulled over to the side of the road and waited for the police car to catch up with him.

Pulling in behind him, the police officer walked up to the driver's side of the BMW, looked at his watch and said, 'Sir, my shift ends in ten minutes. Today is Friday and I'm taking off for the weekend. If you can give me a reason why you were speeding that I've never heard before, I'll let you go.'

The man looked very seriously at the policeman, and replied, 'Years ago, my wife ran off with a policeman. I thought you were bringing her back.'

'Have a good day, Sir,' said the policeman.

No Excuse Sunday

An excerpt from a church bulletin:

To make it possible for everyone to attend church next Sunday, we are going to have a special 'No Excuse Sunday'.

Beds will be placed in the foyer for those who say, 'Sunday is my only day to sleep in.'

We will have blankets for those who think the church is too cold, and fans for those who say it is too hot.

We will have hearing aids for those who say, 'The Priest talks too softly,' and cotton wool for those who say he preaches too loudly.

There will be score cards for those who wish to list hypocrites present.

Some relatives will be in attendance for those who like to go visiting on Sundays.

There will be TV dinners for those who can't go to church and cook dinner also.

One section will be devoted to trees and grass for those who like to see God in nature.

Finally, the Sanctuary will be decorated with both Christmas poinsettias and Easter lilies for those who have never seen the church without them.

Expectations

While ferrying workers back and forth from our company's offshore oil rig, the helicopter I was riding in lost power and went down. Fortunately, we touched down safely on the sea just a few hundred yards from the shore.

The man next to me whipped off his seat-belt, grabbed a safety vest and threw it on, then struggled to get the exit door open.

'Don't jump!' the pilot called out to him. 'This thing is supposed to float!'

As the man threw open the door and jumped out, he yelled back over his shoulder, 'Yeah? It's supposed to *fly*, too!'

Experience

We think if we can disperse adequate information, people will be convinced that Jesus is the way, the truth, and the life, and turn to him. Those methods don't work any longer. I'm not sure they ever did. People aren't looking for information about God. They want to experience God himself. Information leaves them bored, uninterested. Experience, especially the ultimate experience any human being can ever have, leaves them breathless. And that's exactly what we have to offer.

Mark Tabb

Failure

I cannot give you the formula for success but I can give you the formula for failure, which is: try to please everybody.
Herbert Bayard Swope

Faith

Having a clear faith, according to the credo of the church, is often labelled as fundamentalism. Yet relativism – that is, letting oneself be carried here and there by any wind of doctrine – appears as the sole attitude good enough for modern times.

Pope Benedict XVI

Feed your faith, and your doubts will starve to death.

F. F. Bosworth, a great faith preacher some years ago, said that most Christians feed their bodies three hot meals a day but give their spirits just one cold snack a week, and then wonder why they are so weak in faith!

Families

Children in families are like flowers in a bouquet: there's always one determined to face in an opposite direction from the way the arranger desires.

Marcelene Cox

Fathers

A father passing by his son's bedroom was astonished to see the bed was nicely made, and everything was picked up. Then, he saw an envelope, propped up prominently on the pillow. It was addressed, 'Dad'. With the worst premonition, he opened the envelope and read the letter, with trembling hands:

Dear Dad,

It is with great regret and sorrow that I'm writing to you. I had to elope with my new girlfriend, because I wanted to avoid a scene with Mum and you.

I've been finding real passion with Stacy, and she is so nice, but I knew you would not approve of her, because of all her piercings, her tattoos, her tight motorcycle clothes, and because she is so much older than I am.

But it's not only the passion, Dad. She's pregnant. Stacy said that we will be very happy. She owns a trailer in the woods, and has a stack of firewood for the whole winter. We share a dream of having many more children.

Stacy has opened my eyes to the fact that marijuana doesn't really hurt anyone. We'll be growing it for ourselves, and trading it with the other people in the commune, for all the cocaine and ecstasy we want.

In the meantime, we'll pray that science will find a cure for AIDS, so Stacy can get better. She sure deserves it! Don't worry Dad, I'm fifteen, and I know how to take care of myself.

Someday, I'm sure we'll be back to visit, so you can get to know your many grandchildren.

Love, your son,
Joshua.

P.S. Dad, none of the above is true. I'm over at Jason's house. I just wanted to remind you that there are worse things in life than the school report that's on the kitchen table.

Call when it is safe for me to come home.

What happens to children deprived of their natural fathers?

Compared to children in male-headed traditional families where their natural parents are married to each other, children living in female-headed single-parent, lesbian or other environments where they are deprived of their natural fathers are:

- Eight times more likely to go to prison.
- Five times more likely to commit suicide.
- Twenty times more likely to have behavioral problems.
- Twenty times more likely to become rapists.
- 32 times more likely to run away.
- Ten times more likely to abuse chemical substances.
- Nine times more likely to drop out of high school.
- 33 times more likely to be seriously abused.
- 73 times more likely to be fatally abused.
- One-tenth as likely to get A's in school.
- On average have a 44% higher mortality rate.
- On average have a 72% lower standard of living.

From The Garbage Generation *by Daniel Amneus*

Fear

Blessed is that communion with God which renders us impervious to midnight frights, and horrors born of darkness. Not to be afraid is in itself an unspeakable blessing, since for every suffering which we endure from real injury we are tormented by a thousand griefs which arise from fear only. The shadow of the Almighty removes all gloom from the shadow of night: once covered by the divine wing, we care not what winged terrors may fly abroad in the earth.

C. H. Spurgeon

Films

For all the negatives that can be said about the movies, what can be said that is positive of almost all movies is that they reflect, at a very fundamental level, the longings of the soul: the longing that good triumph over evil, that truth wins out, that the drama of life brings out the hero in us, that a good character in the course of a drama grows better, wiser, more understanding, and that a bad character, if not redeemed, is at least brought to justice, and that in the end there is a happy ending which is none other than a dim reflection, I think, of our longing for heaven.

It is without question an incredibly powerful art form, and it is that because it speaks to those longings. It doesn't always speak politely or eloquently or even accurately, but it does speak to the deepest places of the soul.

Ken Gire

Folly

April Fools' Day

In 1957 the respected BBC news show *Panorama* announced that thanks to a very mild winter and the virtual elimination of the dreaded spaghetti weevil, Swiss farmers were enjoying a bumper spaghetti crop. It accompanied this announcement with footage of Swiss peasants pulling strands of spaghetti down from trees. Huge numbers of viewers were taken in, and many called up wanting to know how they could grow their own spaghetti trees. To this question, the BBC diplomatically replied that they should 'place a sprig of spaghetti in a tin of tomato sauce and hope for the best.'

In 1977 the British newspaper *The Guardian* published a special seven-page supplement in honour of the tenth anniversary of San Serriffe, a small republic located in the Indian Ocean consisting of several semi-colon-shaped islands. A series of articles affectionately

described the geography and culture of this obscure nation. Its two main islands were named Upper Caisse and Lower Caisse. Its capital was Bodoni, and its leader was General Pica. *The Guardian*'s phones rang all day as readers sought more information about the idyllic holiday spot. Few noticed that everything about the island was named after printer's terminology. The success of this hoax is widely credited with launching the enthusiasm for April Foolery that then gripped the British tabloids in the following decades.

In 1976 the British astronomer Patrick Moore announced on BBC Radio 2 that at 9:47 a.m. a once-in-a-lifetime astronomical event was going to occur that listeners could experience in their very own homes. The planet Pluto would pass behind Jupiter, temporarily causing a gravitational alignment that would counteract and lessen the Earth's own gravity. Moore told his listeners that if they jumped in the air at the exact moment that this planetary alignment occurred, they would experience a strange floating sensation. When 9:47 a.m. arrived, BBC2 began to receive hundreds of phone calls from listeners claiming to have felt the sensation. One woman even reported that she and her eleven friends had risen from their chairs and floated around the room.

Forgiveness

We shall never understand the extent of God's love in Christ at the Cross until we understand that we shall never have to stand before the judgment of God for our sins. All our sins – without exception – were placed on Christ, and He took the judgment we deserve. He finished the work of redemption.

Once while crossing the North Atlantic in a ship, I looked out my porthole when I got up in the morning and saw one of the blackest clouds I had ever seen. I was certain that we were in for a terrible storm. I ordered my breakfast sent to my room and spoke to the steward about the storm. He said, 'Oh, we've already come through that storm. It's behind us.'

If we are believers in Jesus Christ, we have already come through the storm of judgment. It happened at the Cross. Don't be bound by your guilt or your fears any longer, but realize that sin's penalty has already been paid by Christ – completely and fully.

Billy Graham

Many promising reconciliations have broken down because, while both parties came prepared to forgive, neither party came prepared to be forgiven.

Charles Williams

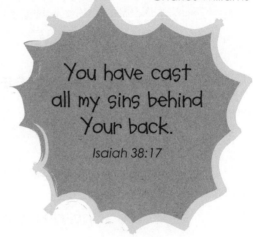

You have cast all my sins behind Your back.

Isaiah 38:17

Sometimes, faith helps ordinary men and women do the humanly impossible: to forgive, to love, to heal, and to redeem. It makes no sense. It is the most sensible thing in the world. The Amish have turned this occasion of spectacular evil into a bright witness to hope. Despite everything, a light shines in the darkness, and the darkness did not overcome it.

Rod Dreher, Dallas Morning News (writing about the Amish school shooting, October 2006)

One Sunday during his sermon, a preacher asks the congregation how many are willing to forgive their enemies. They all raise their hands, except for one elderly lady in the back pew.

The preacher notices and asks, 'Mrs Jones, why aren't you willing to forgive your enemies?'

'Well, I don't have any,' she replies.

'Mrs Jones, you're ninety-three years old and have no enemies? How is this possible?'

'It's easy,' she says. 'I simply outlived all of 'em!'

Freedom

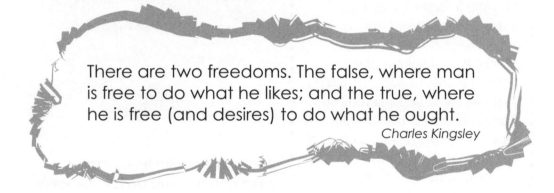

There are two freedoms. The false, where man is free to do what he likes; and the true, where he is free (and desires) to do what he ought.

Charles Kingsley

Friendship

To be resident but alien is a formula for loneliness that few of us can sustain… Christians can survive only by supporting one another through the countless small acts through which we tell one another we are not alone, that God is with us. Friendship is not, therefore, accidental to the Christian life.

Stanley Hauerwas and William Willimon

Funerals

As a young minister, I was asked by a funeral director to hold a graveside service for a homeless man, with no family or friends, who had died while travelling through the area. The funeral was to be held at a cemetery way out in the country, and this man would be the first to be laid to rest there.

As I was not familiar with the backwoods area, I became lost; and being a typical man, I did not stop for directions. I finally arrived an hour late.

I saw the crew, eating lunch, but the hearse was nowhere in sight. I apologized to the workers for my tardiness, and stepped to the side of the open grave, where I saw the vault lid already in place. I assured the workers I would not delay them long.

The workers gathered around, still eating their lunch. I poured out my heart and soul. As I preached, the workers began to say 'Amen,' 'Praise the Lord,' and 'Glory.' I preached, and I preached, like I'd never preached before: from Genesis all the way to Revelation.

I closed the lengthy service with a prayer and walked to my car. I felt I had done my duty for the homeless man and that the crew would leave with a renewed sense of purpose and dedication, in spite of my tardiness.

As I was opening the door and taking off my coat, I overheard one of the workers saying to another, 'I ain't never seen anything like this before... and I've been putting in septic tanks for twenty years.'

Future

Don't worry about the future – worry quenches the work of God within you. The future belongs to God. He is in charge of all things. Never second-guess him.

François Fénelon

Gifts

Presents you don't want to give your wife

- A car-wash kit.
- A table-saw.
- Two all-day passes to Comet's Home Theatre Installation Seminar.
- A case of oil.
- A five-year subscription to *Sports Illustrated*.
- A custom-engraved cricket bat.
- A new outboard motor for a fishing boat.
- The *Rambo* trilogy on DVD.
- A new satellite dish with a sports package.
- A three-year membership of Weight-Watchers Clinic.

Presents you don't want to give your husband

- The *Anne of Avonlea/Anne of Green Gables* Collector's Edition with 74 minutes of extra footage.
- Any knick-knack.
- Tickets to the ballet.
- Yet another tie.
- A Body Shop soap basket.
- Teddy bear pyjamas.
- A vacuum cleaner.
- A weekend seminar on 'Getting in Touch With Your Feelings'.
- A pair of fuzzy bunny slippers.
- A nose/ear-hair trimmer (OK, well maybe).

Giving

The Salvation Army realized that it had never received a donation from the city's most successful lawyer. So a Salvation Army volunteer paid the lawyer a visit in his lavish office.

The volunteer opened the meeting by saying, 'Our research shows that even though your annual income is over $2 million, you don't give a penny to charity. Wouldn't you like to give something back to your community through the Salvation Army?'

The lawyer thought for a minute and said, 'First, did your research also show you that my mother is dying after a long, painful illness and she has huge medical bills that are far beyond her ability to pay?'

Embarrassed, the volunteer mumbled, 'Uh…no, I didn't know that.'

'Secondly,' said the lawyer, 'my brother, a returned serviceman, is blind and confined to a wheelchair and is unable to support his wife and six children.'

The stricken volunteer began to stammer an apology, but was cut off again.

'Thirdly, did your research also show you that my sister's husband died in a dreadful car accident, leaving her penniless with a mortgage and three children, one of whom is disabled, and another has learning disabilities requiring an array of private tutors?'

The humiliated volunteer, completely beaten, said, 'I'm sorry, I had no idea!'

And the lawyer said, 'So… if I didn't give any money to them, what makes you think I'd ever give any to you?'

God

Don't tell God how big your storm is. Tell the storm how big your God is!

A man went to a barbershop to have his hair cut and his beard trimmed. As the barber began to work, they began to have a good conversation.

They talked about many things and various subjects. When they eventually touched on the subject of God, the barber said: 'I don't believe that God exists.'

'Why do you say that?' asked the customer.

'Well, you just have to go out in the street to realize that God doesn't exist. Tell me, if God exists, would there be so many sick people? Would there be abandoned children? If God existed, there would be neither suffering nor pain. I can't imagine a loving God who would allow all of these things.'

The customer thought for a moment, but didn't respond because he didn't want to start an argument. The barber finished his job and the customer left the shop.

Just after he left the barbershop, he saw a man in the street with long, stringy, dirty hair and an untrimmed beard. He looked dirty and unkempt.

The customer turned back and entered the barbershop again and he said to the barber: 'You know what?'

'Barbers do not exist.'

'How can you say that?' asked the surprised barber. 'I am here, and I am a barber. And I just worked on you!'

'No!' the customer exclaimed. 'Barbers don't exist because if they did, there would be no people with dirty, long hair and untrimmed beards, like that man outside.'

'Ah, but barbers *do* exist! What happens is, people do not come to me.'

'Exactly!' affirmed the customer. 'That's the point! God, too, *does* exist! What happens is, people don't go to him and do not look for him. That's why there's so much pain and suffering in the world.'

Grace

Grace is everything for nothing to those who don't deserve anything.

Grace means there is nothing we can do to make God love us more – no amount of spiritual calisthenics and renunciations, no amount of knowledge gained from seminaries, no amount of crusading on behalf of righteous causes. And grace means there is nothing we can do to make God love us less – no amount of racism or pride or pornography or adultery or even murder. Grace means that God already loves us as much as an infinite God can possibly love.

Philip Yancey

An atheist once said, 'If there really is a God, may he prove himself by striking me dead right now.'

Nothing happened.

The atheist proudly announced, 'You see, there is no God!'

His friend responded, 'You've only proved that he is a gracious God.'

During a British conference on comparative religions, experts from around the world debated what, if any, belief was unique to the Christian faith. They began eliminating possibilities. Incarnation? Other religions had different versions of gods appearing in human form. Resurrection? Again, other religions had accounts of return from death.

The debate went on for some time until C. S. Lewis wandered into the room. 'What's the [commotion] about?' he asked, and heard in reply that his colleagues were discussing Christianity's unique contribution among world religions. Lewis responded, 'Oh, that's easy. It's grace.'

A man dies and goes to heaven. Of course, St Peter meets him at the pearly gates.

St Peter says, 'Here's how it works. You need 100 points to make it into heaven. You tell me all the good things you've done, and I give you a certain number of points for each item, depending on how good it was. When you reach 100 points, you get in.'

'OK,' the man says. 'I was married to the same woman for fifty years and never cheated on her, even in my heart.'

'That's wonderful,' says St Peter. 'That's worth three points!'

'Three points?' he says. 'Well, I attended church all my life and supported its ministry with my tithe and service.'

'Terrific!' says St Peter. 'That's certainly worth a point.'

'One point? Golly. How about this: I started a soup kitchen in my city and worked in a shelter for homeless veterans.'

'Fantastic – that's good for two more points.'

'*Two points?!*' the man cries. 'At this rate the only way I'll get into heaven is by the grace of God!'

'Come on in!'

The arms of God be around my shoulders,
the touch of the Holy Spirit upon my head,
the sign of Christ's cross upon my forehead,
the sound of the Holy Spirit in my ears,
the fragrance of the Holy Spirit in my nostrils,
the vision of heaven's company in my eyes,
the conversation of heaven's company on my lips,
the work of God's church in my hands,
the service of God and the neighbour in my feet,
a home for God in my heart,
and to God, the Father of all, my entire being.
Amen.

St Fursey

Hell

The following is an actual question given in a University of Washington Chemistry exam. The answer by one student was so profound that the professor shared it with colleagues:

Bonus Question:

Is Hell exothermic (gives off heat) or endothermic (absorbs heat)?

Most of the students wrote proofs of their beliefs using Boyle's Law (gas cools off when it expands and heats up when it is compressed) or some variant. One student, however, wrote the following:

> First, we need to know how the mass of Hell is changing in time, so we need to know the rate that souls are moving into Hell and the rate they are leaving. I think that we can safely assume that once a soul gets to Hell, it will not leave.

> Therefore, no souls are leaving. As for how many souls are entering Hell, let's look at the different religions that exist in the world today. Most of these religions state that if you are not a member of their religion, you will go to Hell. Since there are more than one of these religions and since people do not belong to more than one religion, we can project that all souls go to Hell.

With birth and death rates as they are, we can expect the number of souls in Hell to increase exponentially. Now, we look at the rate of change of the volume in Hell because Boyle's Law states that in order for the temperature and pressure in Hell to stay the same, the volume of Hell has to expand proportionately as souls are added. This yields two possibilities:

(1) If Hell is expanding at a slower rate than the rate at which souls enter Hell, then the temperature and pressure in Hell will continue to increase until all Hell breaks loose.

(2) If the volume of Hell is expanding at a rate faster than the increase of the volume of souls in Hell, then the temperature and pressure will drop until Hell freezes over.

So which is it?

If we accept the postulate given to me by a girl called Teresa during my first year, that 'It will be a cold day in Hell before I go out with you', and take into account the fact that I still have not succeeded in dating her, then (2) above cannot be true, and thus I am sure that Hell is exothermic and will not freeze over.

This student received the only 'A' grade.

A college drama group presented a play in which one character would stand on a trapdoor and announce, 'I descend into hell!' A stagehand below would then pull a rope, the trapdoor would spring, and the actor would drop from view.

When the actor playing the part became ill, another actor who was quite overweight took his place. When the new actor announced, 'I descend into hell!' the stagehand pulled the rope, and the actor began his plunge, but became hopelessly stuck. No amount of tugging on the rope could make him descend.

One student in the balcony jumped up and yelled: 'Hallelujah! Hell is full!'

Helping

A troop of Boy Scouts was being used as 'guinea pigs' in a test of emergency systems. A mock earthquake was staged, and the Scouts impersonated wounded persons who were to be picked up and cared for by the emergency units.

One Scout was supposed to lie on the ground and await his rescuers, but the first-aid people got behind schedule, and the Scout lay 'wounded' for several hours.

When the first-aid squad arrived where the casualty was supposed to be, they found nothing but a brief note:

'Have bled to death and gone home.'

Holiness

This life, therefore, is not godliness but the process of becoming godly, not health but getting well, not being but becoming, not rest but exercise. We are not now what we shall be, but we are on the way. The process is not yet finished, but it is actively going on. This is not the goal, but it is the right road. At present, everything does not gleam and sparkle, but everything is being cleansed.

Martin Luther

Honesty

It was the last day of a writers' conference and we gathered in one of the dormitories. In our pyjamas we all looked alike. One by one we shared. After the introduction of two authors with published books, and others with claim to fame, it was my turn.

'My name is Ruth,' I said, 'and I feel inferior. I think I'll just go back to my room.' Everybody laughed, so I ploughed ahead. 'I guess you could call me a producer. In the last 30 years I've produced a well-adjusted respiratory therapist, a machinist and another happy homemaker. I'm also involved in the co-production of seven grandchildren.'

I told them how full my life was. Full of checking on cows, helping to fix fences and praying it would stop raining. I told them of busy hours spent babysitting and contending with my household. Then I told them how hungry I was. Hungry for the type of spiritual and emotional food I received at this conference.

From the far corner of the room a quiet girl spoke up. 'Would you please turn so that I can look at you?' she asked. I did, and she continued. 'I want to remember your face when I write,' she said. 'I want to write for people just like you.'

Suddenly I had no need of title or degree. I served a purpose. With her words she helped me realize what I should have known all along: God doesn't make nobodies – everybody is somebody important to Him! So, dare to be yourself. After all, who's better qualified?

Ruth Lee

· Hope

Fear can hold you prisoner. Hope can set you free.

The Shawshank Redemption (1994)

Before the collapse of the Soviet Union, the Russian author Alexander Solzhenitsyn spent many years in the prison camps of Siberia. Along with other prisoners, he worked in the fields day after day, in rain and sun, during summer and winter. His life appeared to be nothing more than backbreaking labour and slow starvation. The intense suffering reduced him to a state of despair.

On one particular day, the hopelessness of his situation became too much for him. He saw no reason to continue his struggle, no reason to keep on living. His life made no difference in the world. So he gave up.

Leaving his shovel on the ground, he slowly walked to a crude bench and sat down. He knew that at any moment a guard would order him to stand up, and when he failed to respond, the guard would beat him to death, probably with his own shovel. He had seen it happen to other prisoners.

As he waited, head down, he felt a presence. Slowly he looked up and saw a skinny old prisoner squat down beside him. The man said nothing. Instead, he used a stick to trace in the dirt the sign of the Cross. The man then got back up and returned to his work.

As Solzhenitsyn stared at the Cross drawn in the dirt his entire perspective changed. He knew he was only one man against the all-powerful Soviet empire. Yet he knew there was something greater than the evil he saw in the prison camp, something greater than the Soviet Union. He knew that hope for all people was represented by that simple Cross. Through the power of the Cross, anything was possible.

Solzhenitsyn slowly rose to his feet, picked up his shovel, and went back to work. Outwardly, nothing had changed. Inside, he had received hope.

Luke Veronis

The optimist says, 'The cup is half full.' The pessimist says, 'The cup is half empty.' The child of God says, 'My cup runneth over...'

Hope is one of the Theological virtues. This means that a continual looking forward to the eternal world is not (as some modern people think) a form of escapism or wishful thinking, but one of the things a Christian is meant to do. It does not mean that we are to leave the present world as it is. If you read history you will find that the Christians who did the most for the present world were just those who thought most of the next... all left their mark on Earth, precisely because their minds were occupied with Heaven. It is since Christians have largely ceased to think of the other world that they have become so ineffective in this. Aim at Heaven and you will get Earth 'thrown in': aim at Earth and you will get neither.

C. S. Lewis

Hospitals

An old man was brought into the hospital after an accident in the street. 'Have you any money to pay for your treatment?' he was asked.

'No.'

'Have you any family who could pay?'

'No.'

'What, no brothers or sisters?'

'No – well, I do have a kid sister, but she has no money.'

'Is she married?'

'Actually, she's a nun.'

'Oh, then she's married to the church.'

'Ah,' said the old man, 'then send the bill to my brother-in-law.'

The comments below really were written on hospital charts:

- The patient refused post mortem.
- The patient has no previous history of suicides.
- Patient has left white blood cells at another hospital.
- Patient's medical history has been remarkably insignificant with only a 40-pound weight gain in the past three days.
- She has no rigors or shaking chills, but her husband states she was very hot in bed last night.
- Patient has chest pain if she lies on her left side for over a year.
- On the second day the knee was better and on the third day it disappeared.
- The patient is tearful and crying constantly. She also appears to be depressed.

- The patient has been depressed since she began seeing me in 1993.
- Discharge status: Alive, but without my permission.
- Healthy-appearing decrepit 69-year-old male, mentally alert, but forgetful.
- Patient had waffles for breakfast and anorexia for lunch.
- She is numb from her toes down.
- While in A&E, she was examined, X-rated and sent home.
- The skin was moist and dry.
- Occasional, constant, infrequent headaches.
- Patient was alert and unresponsive.
- Rectal examination revealed a normal-size thyroid.
- She stated that she had been constipated for most of her life until she got a divorce.
- I saw your patient today, who is still under our car for physical therapy.
- Both breasts are equal and reactive to light and accommodation.
- Examination of genitalia reveals that he is circus sized.
- The lab test indicated abnormal lover function.
- Skin: somewhat pale, but present.
- The pelvic exam will be done later on the floor.
- Large brown stool ambulating in the hall.
- Patient has two teenage children, but no other abnormalities.
- When she fainted, her eyes rolled around the room.
- The patient was in his usual state of good health until his airplane ran out of gas and crashed.
- Between you and me, we ought to be able to get this lady pregnant.
- She slipped on the ice and apparently her legs went in separate directions in early December.
- Patient was seen in consultation by Dr Smith, who felt we should sit on the abdomen and I agree.
- The patient was to have a bowel resection. However, he took a job as a stock broker instead.

Humility

Humility is to make a right estimate of one's self.

C. H. Spurgeon

None are so empty as those who are full of themselves.

Benjamin Whichcote

There are a billion people in China. It's not easy to be an individual in a crowd of more than a billion people. Think of it. More than a *billion* people. That means even if you're a one-in-a-million type of guy, there are still a thousand guys exactly like you.

A. Whitney Brown

It is always the secure who are humble.

G. K. Chesterton

What kills a skunk is the publicity it gives itself.

Abraham Lincoln

We are all worms, but I do believe I am a glow-worm.

Winston Churchill

A man wrapped up in himself makes a very small bundle.

Benjamin Franklin

Humour

Give me a sense of humour, Lord.
Give me the grace to see a joke,
To get some humour out of life,
And pass it on to other folk!

Humour does make romantic relationships more stable. According to a 2007 survey, those couples where both partners said the other had a good sense of humour reported 67 per cent less conflict than couples who thought neither had a good sense of humour.

David Niven

Identification

I like the story of a fifth-grade class at a School in California that had fourteen boys who had no hair. Only one, however, had no choice in the matter. Ian O'Gorman was undergoing chemotherapy for lymphoma, and all his hair was falling out… so he had his head shaved. But then thirteen of his classmates shaved their heads, so Ian wouldn't feel out of place.

Ten-year-old Kyle Hanslik started it all. He talked to some other boys, and before long they all went to the barbershop. 'The last thing he would want is to not fit in,' said Kyle. 'We just wanted to make him feel better.'

Idols

The idols of today are unmistakable – self-esteem without effort, fame without achievement, sex without consequences, wealth without responsibility, pleasure without struggle and experience without commitment.

Rabbi Dr Jonathan Sacks

Incarnation

The teacher was trying desperately to get three twelve-year-old boys to act out the parts of the three kings, but with little success. When they got to the crib where the pretend baby was lying, each boy in turn showed awkwardness and embarrassment. The teacher, too, was growing more and more frustrated as she tried and tried again.

'This time,' she said, 'as you come and look at the baby, say something – the kind of thing people say at home when they see a baby.'

The first and the second boys just couldn't get it right. Then came the third boy and, looking into the crib, he said: 'Oh, isn't he like his father!'

('He that has seen Me has seen the Father also.')

Once upon a time, there was a good and kind king who had a great kingdom with many cities. In one distant city, some people took advantage of the freedom the king gave them and started doing evil. They profited by their evil and began to fear that the king would interfere and throw them in jail. Eventually, these rebels seethed with hatred for the king. They convinced the city that everyone would be better off without the king, and the city declared its independence from the kingdom.

But soon, with everyone doing whatever they wanted, disorder reigned in the city. There was violence, hatred, lying, oppression, murder, rape, slavery, and fear. The king thought: *What should I do? If I take my army and conquer the city by force, the people will fight against me. I will have to kill so many of them, and the rest will only submit through fear or intimidation, which will make them hate me and all I stand for even more. How does that help them – to be either dead or imprisoned or secretly seething with rage? But if I leave them alone, they'll destroy each other, and it breaks my heart to think of the pain they're causing and experiencing.*

So the king did something very surprising. He took off his robes and dressed in the rags of a homeless wanderer. Incognito, he entered the city and began living in a vacant lot near a garbage dump. He took up a trade – fixing broken pottery and furniture. Whenever people came to him, his kindness and goodness and fairness and respect were so striking that they would linger just to be in his presence. They would tell him their fears and questions, and ask his advice. He told them that the rebels had fooled them, and that the true king had a better way to live, which he exemplified and taught. One by one, then two by two, and then by the hundreds, people began to have confidence in him and live his way.

Their influence spread to others, and the movement grew and grew until the whole city regretted its rebellion and wanted to return to the kingdom again. But, ashamed of their horrible mistake, they were afraid to approach the king, believing he would certainly destroy them for their rebellion. But the king-in-disguise told them the good news: he was himself the king, and he loved them. He held nothing against them, and he welcomed them back into his kingdom, having accomplished by a gentle, subtle presence what never could have been accomplished through brute force.

Brian McLaren

He came for you! (Christmas Eve)

'God was manifest in the flesh...' (1 Timothy 3:16). He was born in abject poverty, yet a choir of angels filled the heavens with songs of his greatness. A star that astronomers still can't explain to this day became the compass that brought world leaders to worship at his crib.

His birth defied the laws of biology and his death defied the laws of mortality. No miracle is greater than his life and teaching. He owned no cornfields or fisheries, yet he spread a table for 5,000 and had bread and fish left over. He never walked on expensive carpeting, yet when he walked on water it supported him; when he spoke, the wind and the seas obeyed him.

His crucifixion was the crime of all crimes, yet in God's eyes no less a price could have made your redemption possible. When he died, few mourned, yet God hung black crepe over the sun. Those who crucified him never once trembled at what they'd done, yet the earth shook beneath them. Sin couldn't touch him. Decay couldn't claim his body. The soil that was reddened with his blood couldn't claim his dust.

For over three years he preached the gospel, yet he wrote no books, built no cathedrals, and seemingly had no great financial resources. Yet 2,000 years later, he's still the central character of human history, the perpetual theme of Christian preaching, the pivot around which the ages revolve – and the only Redeemer of the human race!

For every other job, God sent a man. But in order to rescue and recycle you, God *became* a man. Aren't you glad?

Insults

An elderly woman walked into a local country church. The friendly sidesman greeted her at the door.

'Where would you like to sit?' he asked politely.

'The front row, please,' she answered.

'You really don't want to do that,' the usher said. 'The vicar is really boring.'

'Do you happen to know who I am?' the woman enquired.

'No,' he said.

'I'm the vicar's mother,' she replied indignantly.

'Do you know who I am?' he asked.

'No,' she said.

'Good,' he answered and walked away.

Integrity

I'm like an old chair needing that stripping process. Every now and then I have to take a really hard look at the illusions I've built up in myself and my society, see what I've gotten myself into. Illusions? Yes, illusions, the excess baggage I carry around, the unnecessary, the socially expected, all that keeps me living off center too long. Stripping myself of all this is an intentional letting go of these illusions. It is a spiritual act of personal forgiveness. God lets us let go. It's hard work to let God forgive me. I have to discover the original under all these coats I've added, strip away all the cynicism and anger I've built up, get rid of the junk I've taken on, defy my disappointments, and find what is real again.

Donna Schaper

Interruptions

There are enough hours in each day to do all that God wants. The secret lies in knowing how to recognize when an interruption is really an intervention. Who knows, the next knock at the door could be from God.

Ian Coffey

Interviews

'Suppose,' says the old salt of a sea captain, testing his new recruit, 'that a sudden storm springs up on your starboard side. What would you do?'

'Throw out an anchor, sir,' says the new sailor.

'And what would you do if another storm sprang up aft?'

'Throw out another anchor, sir,' the raw recruit replies.

'Now,' says the captain, 'a storm springs up forward of the ship. What would you do this time?'

'Throw out another anchor, Captain.'

'Hold on, hold on. Where are you getting all these anchors from?'

'The same place you're getting your storms, sir,' replied the new recruit.

He got to keep his job.

Jesus

It was Palm Sunday and Jesus was coming into Jerusalem. He was riding on a blazing white stallion and kicking up a cloud of dust as he rode along. He was looking for trouble. The people that he passed on his way were in awe of such a beautiful animal but they were even more awestruck by the man who was riding it. As Jesus passed by, you could hear the people say, 'Who was that masked man?'

There were bad guys on the loose and Jesus had a job to do. As he rode into Jerusalem he quickly sized up the situation and formed a plan to capture the ringleader of the troublemakers. His name was Diablo or Satan. There was a short scuffle and Jesus won handily over Diablo. He hog-tied the devil and threw him in jail.

As a large crowd of people gathered to see what the commotion was all about, Jesus mounted his horse and pulled on the reins. The stallion stood on its hind legs, neighed loudly, and pawed the air with its front legs. When it stood as tall as it could stand, Jesus leaned forward in the saddle. Holding the reins with one hand while lifting his white hat in the air with the other, He shouted with a loud voice, 'Hallelujah'.

As Jesus rode off into the sunset, you could hear the William Tell Overture in the background. Du du dunt. Du du dunt. Du du dunt dunt dunt.

Isn't that how you would have done it if you were Jesus? It's how I would have.

Roger Griffith

More than 2,000 years ago there was a man born contrary to the laws of life. He lived in poverty and was reared in obscurity. He did not travel extensively. Only once did he cross the boundary of the country in which he lived; that was during his exile in childhood as a refugee.

He possessed neither wealth nor influence. His relatives were inconspicuous, and had neither training nor formal education.

In infancy he startled a king; in childhood he puzzled doctors; in manhood he ruled the course of nature. He walked upon the waves as if they were pavements, and he hushed the sea to sleep.

He healed the multitudes without medicine and made no charge for his service.

He never wrote a book, and yet all the libraries of the country could not hold the books that have been written about him.

He never wrote a song, and yet he has furnished the theme of more songs than all the songwriters combined.

He never founded a college, but all the schools put together cannot boast of having as many students.

He never marshalled an army, nor drafted a soldier, nor fired a gun; and yet no leader ever had more volunteers who have, under his orders, made more rebels stack arms and surrender without a shot fired.

He never practised psychiatry, and yet he has healed more broken hearts than all the doctors far and near.

Once each week the wheels of commerce cease their turning and multitudes wend their way to worshipping assemblies to pay homage and respect to him.

The names of the past proud statesman of Greece and Rome have come and gone. The names of the past scientists, philosophers and theologians have come and gone; but the name of this Man abounds more and more. Though time has spread more than two thousand years between people of this generation and the scene of his crucifixion, yet he still lives. Herod could not destroy him, and the grave could not hold him.

He began earthly life in a humble stable but now he stands forth upon the highest pinnacle of heavenly glory, proclaimed of God, acknowledged by angels, adored by saints, and feared by devils, as the living Jesus Christ, Lord and Saviour.

He who was the bread of life began his ministry hungry.
He who was the water of life ended his ministry thirsty.
He who was weary is our rest.
He who paid taxes is the king of the universe.
He who was called a devil cast out demons.
He who prayed hears our prayers.
He who wept dries our tears.
He who was sold for thirty pieces of silver redeemed the world.
He who was led as a lamb to the slaughter is our Good Shepherd.

Jesus of the scars…we seek you now,
We must have sight of thorn-marks on your brow,
We must have you, O Jesus of the scars.
The other gods were strong, but you were
    weak.
They rode, but you did stumble to a throne;
But to our wounds, only God's wounds can
    speak,
And not a god has wounds, but you alone.

Edward Stillito

God's answer to human destruction is a Baby and a Cross.

Jesus Christ – a fugitive, misunderstood, rejected, laughed at, betrayed, forsaken, unjustly convicted, and executed.

But not in vain! He is alive!

Jesus never asks us
to go where he has not gone,
to face what he has not faced,
to love anyone he does not love,
or to give anything that he has
    not given.

The pyramids of Egypt are famous because they contain the mummified bodies of ancient Egyptian kings. Westminster Abbey is noted because within its walls there are contained the remains of many nobles and notables. Muhammad's tomb is visited because of the stone coffin and the bones there. Arlington National Cemetery in Washington, DC is revered because it is a resting place for many outstanding Americans. But the Garden Tomb of Jesus is famous because it is empty!

In the eighteenth century Voltaire prophesied that the Bible would become a museum piece within fifty years of his death. It is ironic that Voltaire's own house would subsequently be used by the Geneva Bible Society as their first depot!

Jesus said, 'My words will never pass away.'

Whether you think Jesus was God or not, you must admit he was a first-rate political economist.
George Bernard Shaw (1856–1950)

From my youth onwards I have found in Jesus my great brother.
Martin Buber, Jewish philosopher (1878–1965)

I am an historian, I am not a believer, but I must confess as an historian that this penniless preacher from Nazareth is irrevocably the very centre of history. Jesus Christ is easily the most dominant figure in all history.
H. G. Wells (1866–1946)

Christianity is the only religion on earth that has felt that omnipotence made God incomplete. Christianity alone has felt that God, to be wholly God must be a rebel as well as a king.
G. K. Chesterton (1874–1936)

I cannot say that Jesus was uniquely divine. He was as much God as Krishna, or Rama, or Mohammed, or Zoroaster.
Mahatma Gandhi (1869–1948)

A man who was completely innocent, offered himself as a sacrifice for the good of others, including his enemies, and became the ransom of the world. It was a perfect act.
Mahatma Gandhi (1869–1948)

There is one very serious defect to my mind in Christ's moral character, and that is that he believed in hell... It is a doctrine that put cruelty into the world and gave the world generations of cruel torture; and the Christ of the Gospels, if you could take him as his chroniclers represent him, would certainly have to be considered partly responsible for that.
Bertrand Russell (1872–1970)

In Jesus, God wills to be true God not only in the height but also in the depth – in the depth of human creatureliness, sinfulness and mortality.
Karl Barth, Swiss theologian (1886–1968)

Jesus Christ is to me the outstanding personality of all time, all history, both as Son of God and as Son of Man. Everything he ever said or did has value for us today and that is something you can say of no other man, dead or alive. There is no easy middle ground to stroll upon. You either accept Jesus or reject him.
Sholem Asch, Jewish author (1880–1957)

As a child I received instruction both in the Bible and in the Talmud. I am a Jew, but I am enthralled by the luminous figure of the Nazarene... No one can read the Gospels without feeling the actual presence of Jesus. His personality pulsates in every word. No myth is filled with such life.
Albert Einstein (1879–1955)

Every person is Christ for me, and since there is only one Jesus, that person is the one person in the world at that moment.
Mother Teresa (1910–97)

A man who was merely a man and said the sort of things Jesus said would not be a great moral teacher. He would either be a lunatic – on a level with the man who says he is a poached egg – or else he would be the Devil of Hell. You must make your choice. Either this man was, and is, the Son of God; or else a madman or something worse. You can shut Him up for a fool, you can spit at Him and kill Him as a demon; or you can fall at His feet and call Him Lord and God. But let us not come with any patronizing nonsense about His being a great human teacher. He has not left that open to us. He did not intend to.
C. S. Lewis (1898–1963)

In his own lifetime Jesus made no impact on history. This is something that I cannot but regard as a special dispensation on God's part, and, I like to think, yet another example of the ironical humour which informs so many of his purposes. To me, it seems highly appropriate that the most important figure in all history should thus escape the notice of memoirists, diarists, commentators, all the tribe of chroniclers who even then existed.
Malcolm Muggeridge (1903–90)

He might be described as an underprivileged, working–class victim of political and religious persecution.

Prince Phillip (1921–)

I accept the resurrection of Easter Sunday not as an invention of the community of disciples, but as a historical event. If the resurrection of Jesus from the dead on that Easter Sunday were a public event which had been made known…not only to the 530 Jewish witnesses but to the entire population, all Jews would have become followers of Jesus.

Pinchas Lapide, Jewish scholar (1922–)

An unsurpassed master of the art of laying bare the inmost core of spiritual truth.

Geza Vermes, author (1924–)

If Jesus had been killed 20 years ago, Catholic school children would be wearing little electric chairs around their necks instead of crosses.

Lenny Bruce, American satirist (1925–66)

It is as wholly wrong to blame Marx for what was done in his name, as it is to blame Jesus for what was done in his.

Tony Benn, British politician (1925–)

After the fall of so many gods in this century, this person, broken at the hands of his opponents and constantly betrayed through the ages by his adherents, is obviously still for innumerable people the most moving figure in the long history of mankind.

Hans Küng, German theologian (1928–)

Jesus Christ was an extremist for love, truth and goodness.

Martin Luther King Jr (1929–68)

Jesus was the first socialist, the first to seek a better life for mankind.

Mikhail Gorbachev (1931–)

[Before the tsunami], I thought the Buddha saved us. You know I believed in Buddha, and I would have died for that at one point. Now I only believe in God. I am a changed Jenat, a new Jenat. Salvation came to my house. That's why. I didn't think I would change like this, but that is the power of God.

Sri Lankan woman who accepted Christ after the 2004 tsunami (Baptist Press)

If Jesus came back and saw what was being done in his name, he wouldn't be able to stop throwing up.

Woody Allen (1935–)

2,000 years ago one man got nailed to a tree for saying how great it would be if everyone was nice to each other for a change.

Douglas Adams, author and radical atheist (1952–2001)

Plato, Socrates and Aristotle are dead.
Julius Caesar, Napoleon Bonaparte
And Adolf Hitler are dead.
Cleopatra, Boadicea
and Florence Nightingale are dead.
Leonardo da Vinci, Isaac Newton
And Charles Darwin are dead.
Confucius, Buddha
and Mohammed are dead.
Karl Marx, Sigmund Freud
and Albert Einstein are dead.
Abraham Lincoln, Winston Churchill
And John F. Kennedy are dead.
They were all alive and are now dead.
But Jesus was dead and is alive for evermore!
(Revelation 1:8)

Jesus Christ is the Completer of unfinished people with unfinished work in unfinished times.

Lona Fowler, from 444 Surprising Quotes about Jesus

We're more popular than Jesus now.

John Lennon, Beatle (1940–80)

Justice

While women weep, as they do now, I'll fight; while children go hungry, as they do now, I'll fight; while men go to prison, in and out, in and out, as they do now, I'll fight; while there is a drunkard left, while there is a poor lost girl upon the streets, while there remains one dark soul without the light of God, I'll fight. I'll fight to the very end!

General William Booth

Kissing

Professors of different subjects define the same word in different ways:

- A Professor of Computer Science: 'A kiss is a few bits of love compiled into a byte.'
- A Professor of Algebra: 'A kiss is two divided by nothing.'
- A Professor of Geometry: 'A kiss is the shortest distance between two straight lines.'
- A Professor of Physics: 'A kiss is the contraction of mouth due to the expansion of the heart.'
- A Professor of Chemistry: 'A kiss is the reaction of the interaction between two hearts.'
- A Professor of Zoology: 'A kiss is the interchange of unisexual salivary bacteria.'
- A Professor of Physiology: 'A kiss is the juxtaposition of two orbicular ors muscles in the state of contraction.'
- A Professor of Dentistry: 'A kiss is infectious and antiseptic.'
- A Professor of Accountancy: 'A kiss is a credit because it is profitable when returned.'
- A Professor of Economics: 'A kiss is that thing for which the demand is higher than the supply.'
- A Professor of Statistics: 'A kiss is an event whose probability depends on the vital statistics of 36–24–36.'
- A Professor of Philosophy: 'A kiss is persecution for the child, ecstasy for the youth and homage for the old.'
- A Professor of English: 'A kiss is a noun that is used as a conjunction; it is more common than proper; it is spoken in the plural and it is applicable to all.'
- A Professor of Engineering: 'Uh, What? I'm not familiar with that term.'

Laws

The UK's top ten most ridiculous laws

- It is illegal to die in the Houses of Parliament.
- It is an act of treason to place a postage stamp bearing the British king or queen's image upside down.
- It is illegal for a woman to be topless in Liverpool except as a clerk in a tropical fish store.
- Eating mince pies on Christmas Day is banned.
- If someone knocks on your door in Scotland and requires the use of your toilet, you are required to let them enter.
- In the UK a pregnant woman can legally relieve herself anywhere she wants, including in a policeman's helmet.
- The head of any dead whale found on the British coast automatically becomes the property of the King, and the tail belongs to the Queen.
- It is illegal not to tell the taxman anything you do not want him to know, but legal not to tell him information you do not mind him knowing.

- It is illegal to enter the Houses of Parliament wearing a suit of armour.
- It is legal to murder a Scotsman within the ancient city walls of York, but only if he is carrying a bow and arrow.

Other ridiculous laws

- In Ohio, it is illegal to get a fish drunk.
- In Switzerland, a man may not relieve himself standing up after 10 p.m.
- It is illegal to be blindfolded while driving a vehicle in Alabama.
- In Florida, unmarried women who parachute on a Sunday could be jailed.
- Women in Vermont must obtain written permission from their husbands to wear false teeth.
- In Milan, it is a legal requirement to smile at all times, except during funerals or hospital visits.
- In France, it is illegal to name a pig Napoleon.

Lawyers

A Rabbi, a Hindu and a lawyer were driving late at night in the country when their car expired. They set out to find help, and came to a farmhouse. When they knocked at the door, the farmer explained that he had only two beds, and one of the three had to sleep in the barn with the animals. The three quickly agreed.

The Rabbi said he would sleep in the barn and let the other two have the beds. Ten minutes after the Rabbi left, there was a knock on the bedroom door. The Rabbi entered exclaiming, 'I can't sleep in the barn; there is a pig in there. It's against my religion to sleep in the same room with a pig!'

The Hindu said *he* would sleep in the barn, as he had no religious problem with pigs. However, about five minutes later, the Hindu burst through the bedroom door saying, 'There's a *cow* in the barn! I can't sleep in the same room as a cow! It's against my religion!'

The lawyer, anxious to get to sleep, said he'd go to the barn, as he had no problem sleeping with animals.

In two minutes, the bedroom door burst open and the pig and the cow entered...

A lawyer in Charlotte, North Carolina purchased a box of very rare and expensive cigars and then insured them against fire, among other things. Within a month, having smoked his entire stockpile of these great cigars and without yet having made even his first premium payment on the policy, the lawyer filed claim against the insurance company. In his claim, the lawyer stated the cigars were lost 'in a series of small fires'.

The insurance company refused to pay, citing the obvious reason that the man had consumed the cigars in the normal fashion. The lawyer sued. And *won*. In delivering the ruling, the judge agreed that the lawyer 'held a policy from the company in which it had warranted that the cigars were insurable and also guaranteed that it would insure them against fire, without defining what is considered to be unacceptable fire' and was obligated to pay the claim. Rather than endure a lengthy and costly appeal process, the insurance company accepted the ruling and paid $15,000 to the lawyer for his cigars lost in the 'fires'.

Now for the best part!

After the lawyer cashed the cheque, the insurance company had him arrested on 24 counts of *arson*! With his own insurance claim and testimony from the previous case being used against him, the lawyer was convicted of intentionally burning his insured property and was sentenced to 24 months in jail and a $24,000 fine.

This is a true story and was the First Place winner in the recent Criminal Lawyers Award Contest.

Leaders

A Christian leader who is not willing to serve is not fit to lead.

Bill Donahue and Russ Robinson,
Building a Church of Small Groups (Zondervan, 2001)

Leadership

The best executive is the one who has sense enough to pick good men to do what he wants done, and self-restraint to keep from meddling with them while they do it.

Theodore Roosevelt

The art of leadership is getting somebody else to do something you want done, and making him think he wants to do it.

Dwight D. Eisenhower

Two blind pilots wearing dark glasses board a plane. One is using a guide dog and the other is tapping his way along the aisle with a cane. Nervous laughter spreads through the cabin, but the men enter the cockpit, the door closes and the engines start up. The passengers begin glancing nervously around, searching for some sign that this is just a little practical joke. None is forthcoming.

The plane moves faster and faster down the runway and the people sitting in the window seats realize they're headed straight for the water at the edge of the airport. As it begins to look as though the plane will plough into the water, panicked screams fill the cabin. At that moment, the plane lifts smoothly into the air. The passengers relax and laugh a little sheepishly and soon all retreat into their magazines, secure in the knowledge that the plane is in good hands.

In the cockpit, one of the blind pilots turns to the other and says, 'Ya know, Bob, one of these days, they're gonna scream too late and we're all gonna die.'

In the early days of Saddleback, every time we had church we had to set up and take down. I was talking with Peter Drucker, the number one management consultant in the world, and I told him, 'I have a church full of managers, white collar people, executives. I can't ask them to set up chairs every week.' He said, 'Why not? They need to. Any executive who won't set up chairs isn't worth his salt!' That comes from the number one management consultant in the world. If a person won't set up chairs in his church, he's not much of a leader. We all need to develop a servant's heart.

The secret of leadership is to keep the four guys who hate you away from the five who are undecided.

Rick Warren

Peter Drucker's calling

The man who Jack Welch called 'the greatest management thinker of the last century' died last year.

I met Peter Drucker once. We sat across a table at a dinner in California. He was very deaf and could hardly hear a word I said. But he did hear me ask whether there was a common thread in his many varied careers – journalist, diplomat, teacher, consultant.

'Of course,' he came back immediately. 'At the heart of everything I have done has been the thought of enabling others, getting the roadblocks out of the way... to enable them to become all that they can be.'

That came back to me this week when I read an article in *Fortune* telling of Drucker's influence, and how in later years he gave himself to helping church and non-profit leaders. His admonitions to pastor Rick Warren are fascinating ... and sobering:

> 'The function of management in a church is to make the church more church-like not more business-like. It's to allow you to do what your mission is.'

Many of us have listened to Peter Drucker tell us how to be better managers.

Perhaps he would most want us to learn to be better Christians!

Leighton Ford (2006)

Life

On the first day, God created the dog and said: 'Sit all day by the door of your house and bark at anyone who comes in or walks past. For this, I will give you a life-span of twenty years.'

The dog said: 'That's a long time to be barking. How about only ten years and I'll give you back the other ten?'

So God agreed.

On the second day, God created the monkey and said: 'Entertain people, do tricks, and make them laugh. For this, I'll give you a twenty-year life-span.'

The monkey said: 'Monkey tricks for twenty years? That's a pretty long time to perform. How about I give you back ten like the dog did?'

And God agreed.

On the third day, God created the cow and said: 'You must go into the field with the farmer all day long and suffer under the sun, have calves and give milk to support the farmer's family. For this, I will give you a life-span of sixty years.'

The cow said: 'That's kind of a tough life you want me to live for sixty years. How about twenty and I'll give back the other forty?'

And God agreed again.

On the fourth day, God created man and said: 'Eat, sleep, play, marry, and enjoy your life. For this, I'll give you twenty years.'

But man said: 'Only twenty years? Could you possibly give me my twenty, the forty the cow gave back, the ten the monkey gave back, and the ten the dog gave back – that makes eighty, OK?'

'OK,' said God. 'You asked for it.'

So that is why the first twenty years we eat, sleep, play and enjoy ourselves.

For the next forty years we slave in the sun to support our family. For the next ten years we do monkey tricks to entertain the grandchildren. And for the last ten years we sit on the front porch and bark at everyone. Life has now been explained to you.

Getting what I had desired for so long – success – and finding it didn't equate with actual happiness made me even more unhappy. What is happiness? It's not in being famous or desired by all these people. It must be somewhere else.

Sting

The Bible shows that all of us have a choice. It isn't just a choice between God and the Devil or Heaven and Hell. No, this choice is much more subtle. Each day you and I must choose the kind of treasure to which we will devote our lives. Either we will spend our lives filling our attic and garage with a lifetime of collectibles or we will spend our lives laying up treasures in Heaven (Luke 12:33–34).

Mark Tabb

● ●

Loneliness

I'll never be happy. I believe I'll die alone. I would want it that way. I've been a loner all my life with my secrets and my pain. I'm really lost, but I'm trying to find myself. I just want to escape. I'm really embarrassed with myself and my life. I want to be a missionary. I think I could do that while keeping my dignity... I'm not going to be a Jesus freak. But that's what I'm going to give my life to. I love Jesus and I believe in Jesus, too – and I'm a Muslim. Listen, I got a imam, I got a rabbi, I got a priest, I got a reverend – I got 'em all.

Mike Tyson

● ●

The Lord's Prayer

The phone rang in the office of the Archbishop of Canterbury. It was Kentucky Fried Chicken. 'Archbishop, we will give £100,000 to the church if you change the Lord's Prayer to say, "Give us today our daily chicken."'

'I'm sorry, I can't do that,' replied the ABC. 'It would mean undoing hundreds – thousands – of years of Christian tradition.'

The next week KFC phoned again. 'We will give you £500,000 to change the Lord's Prayer.'

'I'm sorry, these are Christ's own words – I cannot change them.'

The next week KFC phoned again. 'We will give you £10 million.'

'I'm sorry, the words are in the Bible – I cannot change them.'

Finally, KFC phoned a last time. 'We will give you £100 million to change the prayer.'

The ABC thought hard. The money could help a lot of people; it could make the gospel known to the whole country; it really could do a power of good.

'All right,' he replied. 'I will propose the change to the Archbishops' Council and Synod.'

After much thought and prayer, despite the fact that the words were the Lord's own, that it meant changing thousands of years of Christian tradition, that the words are in the Bible, the Council agreed to present the change to General Synod – after all, the money could do a lot of good.

So at the next Synod, the ABC stood up. 'I've got some good news, and some bad news. The good news is that we are being given £100 million. The bad news – I think we've lost the Hovis account.'

Love

What does love mean?

A group of professionals posed this question to a group of 4 to 8 year-olds. The answers they got were broader and deeper than anyone could have imagined:

• When my grandmother got arthritis, she couldn't bend over and paint her toenails anymore. So my grandfather does it for her all the time, even when his hands got arthritis too. That's love.

Rebecca, age 8

• When someone loves you, the way they say your name is different. You just know that your name is safe in their mouth.

Billy, age 4

• Love is when a girl puts on perfume and a boy puts on shaving cologne and they go out and smell each other.

Karl, age 5

• Love is when you go out to eat and give somebody most of your French fries without making them give you any of theirs.

Chrissy, age 6

• Love is what makes you smile when you're tired.

Terri, age 4

• Love is when my Mummy makes coffee for my Daddy and she takes a sip before giving it to him, to make sure the taste is OK.

Danny, age 7

• Love is when you kiss all the time. Then when you get tired of kissing, you still want to be together and you talk more. My Mummy and Daddy are like that. They look gross when they kiss.

Emily, age 8

• Love is what's in the room with you at Christmas if you stop opening presents and listen.

Bobby, age 7

• If you want to learn to love better, you should start with a friend who you hate.

Nikka, age 6
(This planet needs a few million more people like Nikka!)

• Love is when you tell a guy you like his shirt, then he wears it every day.

Noelle, age 7

• Love is like a little old woman and a little old man who are still friends even after they know each other so well.

Tommy, age 6

- During my piano recital, I was on a stage and I was scared. I looked at all the people watching me and saw my Daddy waving and smiling. He was the only one doing that. I wasn't scared any more.
  Cindy, age 8

- My Mummy loves me more than anybody. You don't see anyone else kissing me to sleep at night.
  Clare, age 6

- Love is when Mummy gives Daddy the best piece of chicken.
  Elaine, age 5

- Love is when Mummy sees Daddy smelly and sweaty and still says he is handsomer than Robert Redford.
  Chris, age 7

- Love is when your puppy licks your face even after you left him alone all day.
  Mary Ann, age 4

- I know my older sister loves me because she gives me all her old clothes and has to go out and buy new ones.
  Lauren, age 4

- When you love somebody, your eyelashes go up and down and little stars come out of you.
  Karen, age 7
  (What an imagination!)

- Love is when Mummy sees Daddy on the toilet and she doesn't think it's gross.
  Mark, age 6

- You really shouldn't say 'I love you' unless you mean it. But if you mean it, you should say it a lot. People forget.
  Jessica, age 8

Open your hearts to the love God instils… God loves you tenderly. What he gives you is not to be kept under lock and key, but to be shared.
Mother Teresa

Lying

A guy sees a sign in front of a house: 'Talking Dog for Sale'. He rings the bell and the owner tells him the dog is in the back yard.

The guy goes into the back yard and sees a black mutt just sitting there. 'You talk?' he asks.

'Yep,' the mutt replies.

'So, what's your story?' asks the guy.

The mutt looks up and says, 'Well, I discovered my gift of talking pretty young and I wanted to help the government, so I told the CIA about my gift, and in no time they had me jetting from country to country, sitting in rooms with spies and world leaders, because no one figured a dog would be eavesdropping. I was one of their most valuable spies eight years running. The jetting around really tired me out, and I knew I wasn't getting any younger and I wanted to settle down. So I signed up for a job at the airport to do some undercover security work, mostly wandering near suspicious characters and listening in. I uncovered some incredible dealings there and was awarded a batch of medals. Had a wife, a mess of puppies, and now I'm just retired.'

The guy is amazed. He goes back in and asks the owner what he wants for the dog.

The owner says, 'Ten dollars.'

The guy says, 'This dog is amazing. Why on earth are you selling him so cheap?'

The owner replies, 'He's a big liar. He didn't do any of that stuff.'

Management

11 simple rules for managing people

This was developed by David Packard (one of the founders of Hewlett Packard) in 1958. This would be a great code of practice for any community:

1. Think first of the other fellow. This is *the* foundation – the first requisite – for getting along with others. And it is the one truly difficult accomplishment you must make. Gaining this, the rest will be 'a breeze'.

2. Build up the other person's sense of importance. When we make the other person seem less important, we frustrate his deepest urges. Allow him to feel equality or superiority, and we can easily get along with him.

3. Respect the other man's personality rights. Respect as something sacred the other fellow's right to be different from you. No two personalities are ever moulded by precisely the same forces.

4. Give sincere appreciation. If we think someone has done a thing well, we should never hesitate to let him know it. *Warning:* This does not mean promiscuous use of obvious flattery. Flattery with most intelligent people gets exactly the reaction it deserves – contempt for the egotistical 'phony' who stoops to it.

5. Eliminate the negative. Criticism seldom does what its user intends, for it invariably causes resentment. The tiniest bit of disapproval can sometimes cause a resentment which will rankle – to your disadvantage – for years.

6. Avoid openly trying to reform people. Every man knows he is imperfect, but he doesn't want someone else trying to correct his faults. If you want to improve a person, help him to embrace a higher working goal – a standard, an ideal –

and he will do his own 'making over' far more effectively than you can do it for him.

7. Try to understand the other person. How would you react to similar circumstances? When you begin to see the 'whys' of him you can't help but get along better with him.

8. Check first impressions. We are especially prone to dislike some people on first sight because of some vague resemblance (of which we are usually unaware) to someone else whom we have had a reason to dislike. Follow Abraham Lincoln's famous self-instruction: 'I do not like that man; therefore I shall get to know him better.'

9. Take care with the details. Watch your smile, your tone of voice, how you use your eyes, the way you greet people, the use of nicknames and remembering faces, names and dates. Little things add polish to your skill in dealing with people. Constantly, deliberately think of them until they become a natural part of your personality.

10. Develop genuine interest in people. You cannot successfully apply the foregoing suggestions unless you have a sincere desire to like, respect and be helpful to others. Conversely, you cannot build genuine interest in people until you have experienced the pleasure of working with them in an atmosphere characterized by mutual liking and respect.

11. Keep it up. That's all – just keep it up!

Marriage

Love is blind – marriage is the eye-opener.
Pauline Thomason

A husband is a man who after emptying the ashtray, manages to look as if he had just finished cleaning the whole house.
James Simpson

A husband and wife are shopping in their local Tesco and the husband picks up a crate of Stella and puts it in their trolley.

'What do you think you're doing?' asks his wife.

'They're on offer – only a tenner for twelve cans,' he replies.

'Put them back, we can't afford them,' demands his wife, and so they carry on shopping.

A few aisles further along the woman picks up a £20 jar of face cream and puts it in the trolley.

'What do you think you're doing?' asks the husband.

'It's my face cream. It makes me look beautiful,' replies his wife.

Her husband retorts: 'So does twelve cans of Stella and it's half the price.'

> Try praising your wife; even if it does frighten her at first.
> Billy Sunday

A man complains to his friend, 'I just can't take it any more.'

His friend says, 'Well, what's wrong?'

He replies: 'It's my wife. Every time we have an argument, she gets historical.'

'You mean *hysterical*, don't you?' the friend asks.

'No,' he says, 'I mean *historical*. Every argument we have, she always brings up the past.'

A teacher was giving her pupils a lesson in logic. 'Here is the situation,' she said. 'A man is standing up in a boat in the middle of a river, fishing. He loses his balance, falls in, and begins splashing and yelling for help. His wife hears the commotion, knows he can't swim, and runs down to the bank. Why do you think she ran to the bank?'

A little girl raised her hand and suggested, 'To draw out all his savings?'

In the art of marriage, the little things are big things:

- It's never being too old to hold hands.
- It's remembering to say 'I love you' at least once each day.
- It's never going to sleep angry.
- It's having a mutual sense of values and common objectives.
- It's standing together, facing the world.
- It's forming a circle of love that gathers in the whole family.
- It's speaking words of appreciation and demonstrating gratitude in thoughtful ways.
- It's having the capacity to forgive and forget.
- It's giving each other an atmosphere in which each can grow.
- It's a common search for the good and the beautiful.
- It's not only marrying the right partner, but also being the right partner.

Bob attended a seminar on interpersonal relationships and became convinced that he needed to do a better job of showing appreciation to his wife. So on his way home from work he picked up a dozen long-stem roses and a box of chocolates. He was eager to see how excited his wife would be at this example of appreciation.

As Bob walked in the door with a big grin, he met his wife in the hallway – and she burst into tears.

'What's wrong, honey?' Bob asked.

'It's been a terrible day,' she exclaimed. 'First, Tommy tried to flush a nappy down the toilet. Then the dishwasher stopped working. Sally came home from school with her legs all scratched, and now you come home drunk!'

Mastercard

'There are some things money can't buy. For everything else there's Mastercard.' I'm sure you've all received their applications in the mail.

However, I'm here to advertise a different card. You see, my life is a product for others to see. I'm a card-carrying representative for The Master's Card. That's right, *The Master's Card*.

Let me tell you about it.

There are no finance charges, no payments due. My bill has already been covered…it's a pre-paid deal. I couldn't afford the price, so Jesus stepped in and paid it for me.

My name is written on the card for all to see. It is accessible twenty-four hours a day from anywhere in the world. The Master's Card has so many benefits it's hard to list them all. Let me share some of them with you… you might want to apply for a personal card yourself.

Just for starters, there is *unlimited grace*.

That's right, there is no pre-set limit to the amount of grace you receive from The Master's Card. Have you been looking for love in all the wrong places? Then, look no farther than The Master's Card. It offers the greatest rate on love that has ever been offered.

The Master's Card gives you access to many 'members only' benefits. Want real joy despite the difficulties of life? Apply for The Master's Card. Want a lasting peace? Apply for The Master's Card. Looking for something you can always rely on in a jam? The Master's Card is perfect for you.

Another great thing about The Master's Card is that it never expires and will never be cancelled. Once you're a member, you're a member for life… eternal life, that is. Membership has its privileges, you know.

So why not apply today? It's only a prayer away…

Catherine Majorfor

Medicine

Patient: 'It's been one month since my last visit and I still feel miserable.'

Doctor: 'Did you follow the instructions on the medicine I gave you?'

Patient: 'I sure did. The bottle said "Keep tightly closed."'

Memories

God gave
us memories that we might
have roses in December.

J. M. Barrie

Men

Why men are happier people

- Your last name stays put.
- The garage is all yours.
- Wedding plans take care of themselves.
- Chocolate is just another snack.
- You can be president.
- You can wear a white T-shirt to a water park.
- You can wear *no* T-shirt to a water park.
- Car mechanics tell you the truth.
- The world is your bathroom.
- You never have to drive to another petrol station because 'This one's just too icky.'
- You don't have to stop and think of which way to turn a nut on a bolt.
- Same work, more pay.
- Wrinkles add character.
- Wedding dress – £3,000; tux rental – £70.
- People never stare at your chest when you're talking to them.
- The occasional well-rendered belch is practically expected.
- New shoes don't cut, blister or mangle your feet.
- One mood, *all* the time.
- Phone conversations are over in thirty seconds flat.
- You know stuff about tanks.
- A five-day holiday requires only one suitcase.

- You can open all your own jars.
- You get extra credit for the slightest act of thoughtfulness.
- If someone forgets to invite you, he or she can still be your friend.
- Your underwear is £4.99 for a three-pack.
- Three pairs of shoes are more than enough (one black pair, two sports pairs).
- You almost never have strap problems in public.
- You are unable to see wrinkles in your clothes.
- Everything on your face stays its original colour.
- The same hairstyle lasts for years, maybe decades.
- You only have to shave your face and neck.
- You can play with toys all your life.
- Your belly usually hides your big hips.
- One wallet and one pair of shoes, one colour, all seasons.
- You can wear shorts no matter how your legs look.
- You can 'do' your nails with a pocket knife.
- You have freedom of choice concerning growing a moustache.
- You can do Christmas shopping for 25 relatives, on 24 December, in 45 minutes.

No wonder men are happier!

Men and women

To our valued customers

HSBC Bank is very pleased to inform you that we are installing new 'Drive-thru' cashpoint machines where our customers will be able to withdraw cash without leaving their vehicles. To enable our customers to make full use of these new facilities, we have conducted intensive studies to come up with the appropriate procedure for their use.

Please read the procedures that apply to you (i.e. *male* or *female*) and remember them for when you use our new machines for the first time.

PROCEDURES FOR OUR MALE CUSTOMERS

1. Drive up to the cash machine.
2. Wind down your car window.
3. Insert card into the machine and enter PIN.
4. Enter amount of cash required and withdraw.
5. Retrieve card, cash and receipt.
6. Wind up window.
7. Drive off.

PROCEDURES FOR OUR FEMALE CUSTOMERS

1. Drive up to the cash machine.
2. Reverse back the required distance to align the car window with the cash machine.
3. Restart the stalled engine.
4. Wind down the window.
5. Find handbag, remove all contents onto passenger seat and locate card.
6. Turn the radio down.
7. Attempt to insert your card.
8. Open the car door to allow easier access to the cash machine due to its excessive distance from the car.
9. Insert card.
10. Re-insert card the right way up.
11. Re-enter your handbag to find your diary with your PIN written on the inside back page.
12. Enter PIN.
13. Press 'Cancel' and re-enter correct PIN.
14. Enter amount of cash required.
15. Check makeup in rear-view mirror.
16. Retrieve cash and receipt.
17. Empty handbag again to locate purse and place cash inside.
18. Place receipt in back of cheque book.
19. Re-check makeup.
20. Drive forward 2 metres.
21. Reverse back to cash machine.
22. Retrieve card.
23. Re-empty handbag, locate card holder and place card into the slot provided.
24. Restart stalled engine and pull away.
25. Drive for 2 or 3 miles.
26. Release handbrake.

Women spend two years nine months of their lives getting ready to go out. Meanwhile, men spend three months of their lives waiting for their wives to get ready!

A man said to his wife one day, 'I don't know how you can be so stupid and so beautiful all at the same time.'

The wife responded, 'Allow me to explain it to you. God made me beautiful so you would be attracted to me; God made me stupid so I would be attracted to you!'

A husband read an article to his wife about how many words women use a day – 30,000 compared to a man's 15,000 words.

The wife replied, 'The reason has to be because a woman has to say everything twice.'

The husband then turned to his wife and asked, 'What?'

Minds

The mind is not a vessel to be filled, but a fire to be kindled.
Plutarch

Ministers

Good news: You baptized seven people today in the river.

Bad news: You lost two of them in the swift current.

Good news: The women's group voted to send you a get-well card.

Bad news: The vote passed by 31 to 30.

Good news: The pastor–parish relations committee accepted your job description the way you wrote it.

Bad news: They were so inspired by it that they asked the bishop to send a new minister capable of filling the position.

Good news: The trustees finally voted to add more church parking.

Bad news: They are going to tarmac the front lawn of the parsonage.

Good news: Church attendance rose dramatically in the last three weeks.

Bad news: You were away on holiday.

Good news: Your biggest critic just left your community.

Bad news: He has been appointed as your conference bishop.

Good news: The youth of the church came to your house for a visit.

Bad news: It was in the middle of the night and they were armed with toilet paper and shaving cream.

Good news: The Church Council has agreed to send you to the Holy Land for study.

Bad news: They are waiting for war to break out before sending you.

Misunderstanding

Four brothers left home for college, and they became successful doctors and lawyers and prospered. Some years later, they chatted after having dinner together. They discussed the gifts that they were able to give to their elderly mother who lived far away in another city.

The first said, 'I had a big house built for Mum.'

The second said, 'I had a £50,000 theatre built in the house.'

The third said, 'I had my Mercedes dealer deliver her an SL600.'

The fourth said, 'Listen to this. You know how Mum loved reading the Bible and you know she can't read it any more because she can't see very well. I met this priest who told me about a parrot that can recite the entire Bible. It took twenty priests twelve years to teach him. I had to pledge to contribute £100,000 a year for twenty years to the church, but it was worth it. Mum just has to name the chapter and verse and the parrot will recite it.'

The other brothers were impressed. After the holidays Mum sent out her thank-you notes.

She wrote: 'Milton, the house you built is so huge. I live in only one room, but I have to clean the whole house. Thanks anyway.'

'Marvin, I am too old to travel. I stay home, I have my groceries delivered, so I never use the Mercedes. The thought was good. Thanks.'

'Michael, you gave me an expensive theatre with Dolby sound. It could hold fifty people, but all my friends are dead, I've lost my hearing and I'm nearly blind. I'll never use it. Thank you for the gesture just the same.'

'Dearest Melvin, you were the only son to have the good sense to give a little thought to your gift. The chicken was delicious. Thank you.'

Money

You aren't wealthy until you have something money can't buy.

Garth Brooks

Old man Fielding, the miser, at last went to his reward and presented himself at the Pearly Gates.

St Peter greeted him with appropriate solemnity and escorted him to his new abode.

Walking past numerous elegant mansions, finally they arrived at a dilapidated shack at the end of the street.

Fielding, much taken aback, began, 'Why am I left with a rundown shack when all of these others have fine mansions?'

'Well, sir,' replied St Peter, 'we did the best we could with the money you sent us.'

◇◇

Mothers

Mothers' maintenance manual

Many of us take better care of our cars then we do our mothers, and yet we only expect our cars to last five or six years, but we expect our mothers to last for a lifetime. Maybe we need a maintenance manual for mothers so we would know how to take care of them at least as well as we do our cars. Here are some items that might be included in such a manual.

ENGINE

A mother's engine is one of the most dependable kinds you can find. She can reach top speed from a prone position at a single cry from a sleeping child. But regular breaks are needed to keep up that peak performance. Mothers need a hot bath and a nap every 100 miles, a baby-sitter and a night out every 1,000 miles, and a live-in baby-sitter with a one-week holiday every 10,000 miles.

BATTERY

A mother's batteries should be recharged regularly. Handmade items, notes, unexpected hugs and kisses, and frequent 'I love you's will do very well for a recharge.

CARBURETTOR

When a mother's carburettor floods it should be treated immediately with Kleenex and a soft shoulder.

BRAKES

See that she uses her brakes to slow down often and come to a full stop occasionally. (A squeaking sound indicates a need for a rest.)

FUEL

Most mothers can run indefinitely on coffee, leftovers and salads, but an occasional dinner for two at a nice restaurant will really add to her efficiency.

CHASSIS

Mothers run best when their bodies are properly maintained. Regular exercise should be encouraged and provided for as necessary. A change in hairdo or makeup in spring and autumn are also helpful. If you notice the chassis begins to sag, immediately start a programme of walking, jogging, swimming, or bike-riding. These are most effective when done with fathers.

TUNE-UPS

Mothers need regular tune-ups. Compliments are both the cheapest and most effective way to keep a mother purring contentedly.

Oh yes, and let's not forget to speak to mother lovingly and respectfully, especially when she reminds you to drive carefully and have a good time.

If these instructions are followed consistently, this fantastic creation and gift from God, whom we call 'Mother', should last a lifetime and give good service and constant love to those who need her most.

Being a mum

If motherhood had been presented to us this way, none of us would have done it!

POSITION

Mother, Mom, Mama, Mummy, Ma.

JOB DESCRIPTION

Long-term team players needed for challenging permanent work in an often chaotic environment. Candidates must possess excellent communication and organizational skills and be willing to work variable hours, which will include evenings and weekends and frequent 24-hour shifts on call. Some overnight travel required, including trips to primitive camping sites on rainy weekends and endless sports tournaments in faraway cities. Travel expenses not reimbursed. Extensive courier duties also required.

RESPONSIBILITIES

The rest of your life. Must be willing to be hated, at least temporarily, until someone needs £5. Must be willing to bite tongue repeatedly. Also, must possess the physical stamina of a pack mule and be able to go from 0 to 60 mph in 3 seconds flat in case, this time, the screams from the back yard are not someone just crying wolf.

Must be willing to face stimulating technical challenges, such as small-gadget repair, mysteriously sluggish toilets and stuck zippers.

Must screen phone calls, maintain calendars and coordinate production of multiple homework projects. Must have ability to plan and organize social gatherings for clients of all ages and mental outlooks. Must be willing to be indispensable one minute, an embarrassment the next.

Must handle assembly and product safety testing of a half million cheap, plastic toys and battery-operated devices. Must always hope for the best but be prepared for the worst. Must assume final, complete accountability for the quality of the end product. Responsibilities also include floor maintenance and janitorial work throughout the facility.

POSSIBILITY FOR ADVANCEMENT AND PROMOTION

Virtually none. Your job is to remain in the same position for years, without complaining, constantly retraining and updating your skills, so that those in your charge can ultimately surpass you.

PREVIOUS EXPERIENCE

None required, unfortunately. On-the-job training offered on a continually exhausting basis.

WAGES AND COMPENSATION

Get this! You pay *them*! Offering frequent raises and bonuses. A balloon payment is due when they turn eighteen because of the assumption that college will help them become financially independent. When you die, you give them whatever is left. The oddest thing about this reverse-salary scheme is that you actually enjoy it and wish you could only do more.

BENEFITS

While no health or dental insurance, no pension, no tuition reimbursement, no paid holidays and no stock options are offered, this job supplies limitless opportunities for personal growth and free hugs for life if you play your cards right.

A mother's letter

Dear Son,

Just a few lines to let you know that I am still alive. I am writing this slowly because I know that you can't read fast. You won't know the house when you come home – we've moved.

About your father – he has got a lovely new job. He has 500 men under him. He cuts grass at the cemetery. Your sister Mary had a baby this morning. I haven't found out yet whether it is a boy or a girl so I don't know if you're an aunt or an uncle.

I went to the doctor's on Thursday and your father came with me. The doctor put a small tube in my mouth and told me not to talk for ten minutes. Your father offered to buy it from him.

Your uncle Patrick drowned last week in a vat of Irish whisky at the Dublin brewery. Some of his workmates tried to save him but he fought them off bravely. They cremated him and it took three days to put the fire out.

It only rained twice this week, first for three days then for four days. We had a letter from the undertaker. He said if the last payment on your grandmother's plot wasn't paid in seven days, up she comes.

Your loving mother.

P.S. I was going to send you five pounds but I have already sealed the envelope.

A man received two sweaters for Hanukkah from his mother. The next time he visited her, he made sure to wear one of the two sweaters.

As he entered her home, instead of the expected smile, she said, 'What's the matter? You didn't like the other one?'

Music

The best Country & Western song titles of all time

- 'Her Teeth Was Stained, But Her Heart Was Pure'
- 'Don't Know Whether To Kill Myself Or Go Bowling'
- 'Liked You Better Before I Knew You So Well'
- 'Still Miss You Baby, But My Aim's Gettin' Better'
- 'I'm So Miserable Without You, It's Like Having You Here'
- 'Mama Get A Hammer (There's A Fly On Papa's Head)'
- 'She Got The Ring and I Got The Finger'
- 'You're The Reason Our Kids Are So Ugly'

Nakedness

A minister, a priest and a rabbi went for a hike one day. It was very hot. They were sweating and exhausted when they came upon a small lake. Since it was fairly secluded, they took off all their clothes and jumped in the water.

Feeling refreshed, the trio decided to pick a few berries while enjoying their 'freedom'. As they were crossing an open area, who should come along but a group of ladies from town. Unable to get to their clothes in time, the minister and the priest covered their privates and the rabbi covered his face while they ran for cover.

After the ladies had left and the men got their clothes back on, the minister and the priest asked the rabbi why he covered his face rather than his privates. The rabbi replied, 'I don't know about you, but in my congregation, it's my face they would recognize.'

Nature

I believe in my heart that faith in Jesus Christ can and will lead us beyond an exclusive concern for the well-being of other human beings to the broader concern for the well-being of the birds in our backyards, the fish in our rivers, and every living creature on the face of the earth.

John Wesley (1703–91)

Newspapers

If you don't read the newspapers, you are uninformed. If you do read the newspapers, you are misinformed.

Mark Twain

Normality

During a visit to the mental asylum, a visitor asked the Director how to determine whether or not a patient should be admitted to the asylum.

'Well,' said the Director, 'we fill up a bathtub, then we offer a teaspoon, a teacup and a bucket to the patient and ask him or her to empty the bathtub.'

'Oh, I understand,' said the visitor. 'A normal person would use the bucket because it's bigger than the spoon or the teacup.'

'No,' said the Director, 'a normal person would pull the plug. Do you want a bed near the window?'

Obedience

'You Gentiles have taken everything from us,' argued a Jew.

'Like what?' said the Christian.

'Like the Ten Commandments, for a start.'

'We may have taken them,' the Christian replied, 'but you can never accuse us of keeping them!'

///

Obituary

If Jesus had an obituary

Jesus Christ, 33, of Nazareth, died on Friday on Mount Calvary, also known as Golgotha, the Place of the Skull. Betrayed by the apostle Judas, Jesus was crucified by the Romans, by order of Pontius Pilate. The causes of death were crucifixion, extreme exhaustion, severe torture, and loss of blood.

Jesus Christ, a descendant of Abraham, was a member of the house of David. He was the Son of the late Joseph, a carpenter of Nazareth, and Mary, his devoted mother. Jesus was born in a stable in the city of Bethlehem, Judea. He is survived by his mother, his faithful apostles, numerous disciples, and many other followers.

Jesus was self-educated and spent most of his adult life working as a teacher. Jesus also occasionally worked as a medical doctor and it is reported that he healed many patients. Up until the time of his death, Jesus was teaching and sharing the Good News, healing the sick, touching the lonely, feeding the hungry, and helping the poor.

Jesus was most noted for telling parables about his Father's kingdom and performing miracles, such as feeding over 5,000 people with only five loaves of bread and two fish, and healing a man who was born blind. On the day before his death, he held a Last Supper celebrating the Passover Feast, at which he foretold his death.

The body was quickly buried in a stone grave, which was donated by Joseph of Arimathea, a loyal friend of the family. By order of Pontius Pilate, a boulder was rolled in front of the tomb. Roman soldiers were put on guard.

In lieu of flowers, the family has requested that everyone try to live as Jesus did. Donations may be sent to anyone in need.

Parenting

As Christian parents, we are not to simply socialize our children into civil human beings; we are to train them to advance the Kingdom of God. Christian parenting is less like a cotillion and more like a boot camp. It's not simply about manners and proper decorum in public; it's about being conditioned and prepared to take on life's challenges. It's not about fussing with their collar so they'll look cute at the dance. It's about getting them ready to do battle.

Timothy Smith, The Danger of Raising Nice Kids *(InterVarsity, 2006)*

Peace

I am passing this on to you because it definitely worked for me and we all could use more calm in our lives.

By following the simple advice I heard on a medical TV show, I have finally found inner peace.

A doctor proclaimed that the way to achieve inner peace is to finish all the things you have started.

So I looked around my house to see things I had started and hadn't finished and, before leaving the house this morning, I finished off a bottle of Merlot, a bottle of Shhhardonay, a bodle of Baileys, a butle of vocka, a pockage of Prunglies, tha mainder of bot Prozic and Valum scriptins, the res of the Chesescke an a bax a cholates.

Yu haf no idr who gud I fel.

Peas sen dis orn to dem yu fee ar in ned ov inr pece.

People

The Tate family

- Old man Dictate, who wants to run everything.
- Cousin Rotate, who wants to change everything – again.
- Agitate and Irritate are always stirring up trouble.
- Hesitate and Vegetate always want to leave it till next year.
- Cogitate and Meditate, being Cornish, do things 'drekkly'!
- Aunt Imitate wants everything to be like it was in her old church.
- Young Devastate is a voice of doom.
- Miss Facilitate is always most helpful.
- Dr Amputate has regretfully cut himself off completely.

People are often unreasonable, illogical, and self-centred; forgive them, anyway.

If you are kind, people may accuse you of selfish, ulterior motives; be kind anyway.

If you are successful, you will win some false friends and some true enemies. Succeed anyway.

If you are honest and frank, people may cheat you; be honest and frank anyway.

What you spend years building, someone could destroy overnight; build anyway.

If you find serenity and happiness, they may be jealous; be happy anyway.

The good you do today, people will often forget tomorrow; do good anyway.

Give the world the best you have, and it may never be enough; give the world the best you've got anyway.

You see, in the final analysis, it is between you and God; it was never between you and them anyway.

Mother Teresa

Perseverance

Does the road wind up the hill all the way?
Yes! To the very end.
Will the day's journey take the whole long day?
From morn to night, my friend.

Christina Rossetti
(sent to Winston Churchill by his wife Clementine
during the First World War, after Winston had written
to her saying that he was considering 'deserting')

Perspective

Unless there is within us that which is above us, we shall soon yield to that which is about us.
P. T. Forsyth

Pessimism

A pessimist's blood type is always B-negative.

A pessimist's commentary on Psalm 23, by Ima Whiner

The Lord is my shepherd, I shall not want.

'Shall not want'? Give me a break. I want lots of things. I'd like to have a nicer house, a better job, and a pay raise. I want people to do what I say when I say. And I wouldn't mind winning the lottery either.

He makes me lie down in green pastures; he leads me beside quiet waters.

I have a problem with the words 'makes me'. That sounds a bit legalistic to me. First you say I can't want things; now you're making me do things.

He restores my soul; he guides me in the paths of righteousness for his name's sake.

I don't want to be guided down the paths of righteousness. I prefer the more scenic routes. How about leading me to Hawaii for a change? What about Vegas? I'm getting a little tired of the paths of righteousness. The next thing you know, you'll be leading me through a dark valley.

Even though I walk through the valley of the shadow of death, I fear no evil, for you are with me.

What am I doing walking through the valley of the shadow of

death? I thought I was supposed to be lying down in green pastures. Did you take a wrong turn, or what? And you call yourself a shepherd?

Your rod and your staff, they comfort me.

To tell you the truth, a rod and staff are not my idea of comfort. A rod and reel I'll take. A back massage would be even better. Skip the rod and staff.

You prepare a table before me in the presence of my enemies.

Great. Out of all the restaurants in the world, you choose the one where my enemies like to eat. I'm sure I'll relish every bite of that meal!

You have anointed my head with oil; my cup overflows.

I don't want any oil on my head. I prefer shampoo. And for goodness sake, can't you stop pouring before my cup overflows? What kind of waiter are you anyway? How would you like to have hot coffee spilled all over your hand?

Surely goodness and loving kindness will follow me all the days of my life, and I will dwell in the house of the Lord forever.

I don't want to be confined to a house forever. That sounds like a prison. It might be nice to step outside once every thousand years or so. I never will understand why so many people love the 23rd Psalm.

who threw that roll?!

it's just your enemies dear — ignore them

Phones

The mental health hotline

Hello, and welcome to the mental health hotline.

- If you are obsessive compulsive, press 1 repeatedly.
- If you are co-dependent, ask someone to press 2 for you.
- If you have multiple personality disorder, press 3, 4, 5 and 6.
- If you are paranoid, we know who you are and what you want. Stay on the line so we can trace your call.
- If you are delusional, press 7 and your call will be transferred to the mother ship.
- If you are schizophrenic, listen carefully and a little voice will tell you which number to press.
- If you are depressed, it doesn't matter which number you press – no one will answer you.
- If you are dyslexic, press 9696969696969696969696.
- If you have a nervous disorder, please fidget with the hash key until a representative comes on the line.
- If you have amnesia, press 8 and state your name, address, phone number, date of birth and your mother's maiden name.
- If you have PTSD, slowly and carefully press 000.
- If you have bi-polar disorder, please leave a message after the beep or before the beep.
- Or after the beep. Please wait for the beep.
- If you have a short-term memory loss, press 9.
- If you have a short-term memory loss, press 9.
- If you have a short-term memory loss, press 9.
- If you have a short-term memory loss, press 9.
- If you have low self-esteem please hang up. All our operators are too busy to talk to you.

Pluralism

Hilary Swank, 1999's Oscar winner for Best Actress and wife of actor Chad Lowe, was asked about her and her husband's beliefs. She responded:

> *'It's not like we're Catholic or Christian or Episcopal or practise Judaism or Buddhism even. We just kind of believe in a higher power and that doesn't mean a man God, or someone on a cross. It just means that we all have god-like qualities. We have the power inside of us to do good things. But I don't want you to write it like I'm freaky.'*

//

Potential

Though he began his studies under the tutelage of a noted scholastic philosopher (Albertus Magnus in Paris), Thomas Aquinas made a poor first impression upon his fellow students – who nicknamed him 'the dumb ox'.

One day Magnus invited Aquinas for a private session at which every subject in the university curriculum was passionately discussed. Suitably impressed, Magnus magnanimously sang Aquinas's praises at his following lecture:

> *'You call brother Thomas a dumb ox,' he declared. 'Let me tell you that one day the whole world will listen to his bellowings.'*

\\

Poverty

I was hungry and you formed a committee to investigate my hunger.
I was homeless, and you filed a report on my plight.
I was sick and you held a seminar on the underprivileged.
You have investigated all the aspects of my plight.
And yet I am still hungry, homeless and sick.

David Watson

In the Third World the daily children's death toll is:

- 5,400 from measles
- 4,900 from tetanus
- 1,800 from whooping cough
- 200 from TB, polio or diphtheria

All 12,300 children could live if immunized at the cost of just £1 per child. Life has never been so cheap!

Tear Fund

The exclusion of the weak and insignificant, the seemingly useless people, from a Christian community may actually mean the exclusion of Christ; in the poor brother Christ is knocking at the door.

Dietrich Bonhoeffer

Prayer

A priest, a minister and a guru sat discussing the best positions for prayer, while a telephone repairman worked nearby.

'Kneeling is definitely the best way to pray,' the priest said.

'No,' said the minister. 'I get the best results standing with my hands outstretched to heaven.'

'You're both wrong,' the guru said. 'The most effective prayer position is lying down on the floor.'

The repairman could contain himself no longer.

'Hey, fellas,' he interrupted. 'The best prayin' I ever did was when I was hangin' upside down from a telephone pole.'

Prayer is not designed as an intercom between us and God to serve the domestic comforts of the saints. It's designed as a walkie-talkie for spiritual battlefields. It's the link between active soldiers and their command headquarters, with its unlimited firepower and air cover and strategic wisdom.

John Piper

They walked in tandem, each of the ninety-three students filing into the already crowded auditorium. With rich maroon gowns flowing and the traditional caps, they looked almost as grown up as they felt.

Dads swallowed hard behind broad smiles, and mums freely brushed away tears.

This class would not pray during the commencements – not by choice, but because of a recent court ruling prohibiting it. The principal and several students were careful to stay within the guidelines allowed by the ruling. They gave inspirational and challenging speeches, but no one mentioned divine guidance and no one asked for blessings on the graduates or their families.

The speeches were nice, but they were routine... until the final speech received a standing ovation.

A solitary student walked proudly to the microphone. He stood still and silent for just a moment, and then, it happened.

All ninety-two students, every single one of them, suddenly *sneezed*!

The student on stage simply looked at the audience and said, '*God bless you*, each and every one of you!' And he walked off stage...

The audience exploded into applause. The graduating class had found a unique way to invoke God's blessing on their future, with or without the court's approval.

Aman's daughter had asked the local minister to come and pray with her father. When the minister arrived, he found the man lying in bed with his head propped up on two pillows. An empty chair sat beside his bed.

The minister assumed that the old fellow had been informed of his visit. 'I guess you were expecting me,' he said.

'No, who are you?' said the father.

The minister told him his name and then remarked, 'I saw the empty chair and I figured you knew I was going to show up.'

'Oh yeah, the chair,' said the bed-ridden man. 'Would you mind closing the door?'

Puzzled, the minister shut the door.

'I have never told anyone this, not even my daughter,' said the man. 'But all of my life I have never known how to pray. At church I used to hear the pastor talk about prayer, but it went right over my head.

'I abandoned any attempt at prayer,' the old man continued, 'until one day four years ago, my best friend said to me, "Johnny, prayer is just a simple matter of having a conversation with Jesus. Here is what I suggest. Sit down in a chair; place an empty chair in front of you, and in faith see Jesus on the chair. It's not spooky because he promised, 'I will be with you always.' Then just speak to him in the same way you're doing with me right now."

'So, I tried it and I've liked it so much that I do it a couple of hours every day. I'm careful, though. If my daughter saw me talking to an empty chair, she'd either have a nervous breakdown or send me off to the funny farm.'

The minister was deeply moved by the story and encouraged the old man to continue on the journey. Then he prayed with him, anointed him with oil, and returned to the church.

Later the daughter called to tell the minister that her daddy had died peacefully that same afternoon.

'Did he die in peace?' he asked.

'Yes, when I left the house about two o'clock, he called me over to his bedside, told me he loved me and kissed me on the cheek. When I got back from the store an hour later, I found him dead. But there was something strange about his death. Apparently, just before Daddy died, he leaned over and rested his head on the chair beside the bed. What do you make of that?'

The minister wiped a tear from his eye and said, 'I wish we could all go like that.'

A famous example of a prayer riddled with wrong motives is that of John Ward of Hackney, written in the eighteenth century:

O Lord, thou knowest that I have nine estates in the City of London, and likewise that I have lately purchased one estate in the county of Essex; I beseech thee to preserve the two counties of Essex and Middlesex from fire and earthquake; and as I have a mortgage in Hertfordshire, I beg of thee likewise to have an eye of compassion on that county; and for the rest of the counties thou mayest deal with them as thou art pleased.

O Lord, enable the bank to answer their bills, and make all my debtors good men. Give a prosperous voyage and return to the mermaid ship, because I have insured it; and as thou hast said that the days of the wicked are but short, I trust in thee, that thou wilt not forget thy promise, as I have purchased an estate in reversion which will be mine on the death of that profligate young man, Sir J. L.

Keep my friends from sinking, and preserve me from thieves and housebreakers, and make all my servants so honest and faithful that they may attend to my interests, and never cheat me out of my property, night or day.

Amen.

'With all the work you do,' Cardinal Spellman was asked one day, 'do you ever get so tired that you forget to say your prayers at night?'

'No,' Spellman replied with a smile. 'When I'm so tired I can't keep my eyes open, I simply say: "Dear God, you know I've been working in your vineyard all day. If you don't mind, could we skip the details till morning?"'

Preaching

A Catholic priest, a Pentecostal preacher and a rabbi all served as chaplains to the students of Northern Michigan University in Marquette. They would get together two or three times a week for coffee and to talk shop. One day, someone made the comment that preaching to people isn't really all that hard. A real challenge would be to preach to a bear. One thing led to another, and they decided to do an experiment. They would all go out into the woods, find a bear, preach to it, and attempt to convert it. Seven days later, they all came together to discuss their experience.

Father Flannery, who had his arm in a sling, was on crutches, and had various bandages on his body and limbs, went first. 'Well,' he said, 'I went into the woods to find me a bear. And when I found him, I began to read to him from the Catechism. Well, that bear wanted nothing to do with me and began to slap me around. So I quickly grabbed my holy water, sprinkled him and he became as gentle as a lamb. The bishop is coming out next week to give him first communion and confirmation.'

Reverend Billy Bob spoke next. He was in a wheelchair, had one arm and both legs in casts, and had an IV drip. In his best fire-and-brimstone oratory, he claimed, '*Well*, brothers, you *know* that we don't sprinkle! I went out and I *found* me a bear. And then I began to read to my bear from God's *holy Word*! But that bear wanted nothing to do with me. So I took *hold* of him and we began to wrestle. We wrestled down one hill, *up* another and *down* another until we came to a creek. So I quickly *dunked* him and *baptized* his hairy soul. And just like you said, he became as gentle as a lamb. We spent the rest of the day praising Jesus.'

The priest and the preacher both looked down at the rabbi, who was lying in a hospital bed. He was in a body cast and traction with IVs and monitors running in and out of him. He was in really bad shape. The rabbi looked up and said, 'Looking back on it, circumcision may not have been the best way to start.'

While preaching a sermon one day, John Wesley was dismayed to find that several members of his congregation had fallen asleep.

'Fire! Fire!' he suddenly cried, whereupon the guilty parishioners jumped up with alarm.

'Where?' they demanded, glancing around.

'In hell,' Wesley replied, 'for those who sleep under the preaching of the Word!'

Jesus taught profound truths in simple ways. Today, we do the opposite. We teach simple truths in profound ways.

Rick Warren

Prejudice

A great many people think they are thinking when they are merely rearranging their prejudices.

William James

Priorities

Guard well your spare moments. They are like uncut diamonds. Discard them and their value will never be known. Improve them and they will become the brightest gems in a useful life.

Ralph Waldo Emerson

Pressure

Pressure is nothing more than the shadow of great opportunity.

Michael Johnson

Things which matter most must never be at the mercy of things that matter least.

Johann Wolfgang von Goethe

Professions

A group of teenage lads were discussing their hopes and dreams for the future. The majority had plans for big careers, earning them more than enough income to live on. However, one said he would be pursuing a job in the church. His accomplices derided him, saying that he would never be able to support himself, let alone any family he might get.

'It's true,' he concurred, 'the salary for serving the Lord is highly variable. But,' he wryly added, 'there's a Great Commission.'

Providence

Regardless of the cause, none of your problems could happen without God's permission. Everything that happens to a child of God is Father-filtered, and he intends to use it for good even when Satan and others mean it for bad.

Rick Warren

On a chilly afternoon before going home for dinner, Pastor Walter Klempel fired up the church furnace in preparation for choir practice. When it was time to return to church with his family they were delayed because his daughter changed clothes. At the same time student Ladona Vadergrift was struggling with a geometry problem and stayed home working on it. Sisters Royena and Sadie Estes' car wouldn't start. Herbert Kipf lingered over a letter he'd put off writing. Joyce Black was feeling 'plain lazy' and stayed home till the last minute. Pianist Marilyn Paul fell asleep after dinner and her mum, the choir director, had trouble waking her. Pals Lucille Jones and Dorothy Wood were late because of a radio broadcast. Every single choir member was late; something that's never happened before nor since. Was it just a fluke? No! At 7:30 that night the West Side Church was flattened by an explosion from a gas leak ignited by the furnace... directly below the choir loft!

From The Word for Today *(United Christian Broadcasters)*

The story is told of a king in Africa who had a close friend with whom he grew up. The friend had a habit of looking at every situation that ever occurred in his life (positive or negative) and remarking, 'This is good!'

One day the king and his friend were out on a hunting expedition. The friend would load and prepare the guns for the king. The friend had apparently done something wrong in preparing one of the guns, for after taking the gun from his friend, the king fired it and his thumb was blown off. Examining the situation, the friend remarked as usual, 'This is good!'

To which the king replied, 'No, this is not good!' and proceeded to send his friend to prison. About a year later, the king was hunting in an area that he should have known to stay clear of. Cannibals captured him and took him to their village. They tied his hands, piled some wood, and bound him to a stake.

As they came near to set fire to the wood, they noticed that the king was missing a thumb. Being superstitious, they never ate anyone who was less than whole. So untying the king, they sent him on his way.

As he returned home, he was reminded of the event that had taken his thumb and felt remorse for his treatment of his friend. He went immediately to the prison to speak with his friend. 'You were right,' he said, 'it was good that my thumb was blown off.' And he proceeded to tell the friend all that had just happened. 'And so, I am very sorry for sending you to prison for so long. It was bad for me to do this.'

'No,' his friend replied, 'this is good!'

'What do you mean, "This is good"? How could it be good that I sent my friend to prison for a year?'

'If I had not been in prison, I would have been with you.'

Purpose

Albert Einstein was taking a train to speak at a meeting. The conductor stopped by to punch his ticket, but the great scientist, preoccupied with his work, explained that he couldn't find his ticket. Not in his pockets, not in his briefcase.

The conductor said, 'We all know who you are, Dr Einstein. I'm sure you bought a ticket. Don't worry about it.'

As the conductor moved along, he looked back to see Einstein on his hands and knees searching under the seats for his ticket. The conductor walked back. 'Dr Einstein, please, don't worry about it. I know who you are.'

Exasperated, Einstein looked up and said, 'I, too, know who I am. What I don't know is where I'm going.'

Put downs

The Smithsonian Institute sent the following rejection letter in response to an amateur palaeontologist's submission of a Malibu Barbie head for consideration as a prehistoric find:

Paleoanthropology Division
Smithsonian Institute
207 Pennsylvania Avenue
Washington, DC 20078

Dear Sir:

Thank you for your latest submission to the Institute, labeled '211-D, layer seven, next to the clothesline post. Hominid skull.' We have given this specimen a careful and detailed examination, and regret to inform you that we disagree with your theory that it represents 'conclusive proof of the presence of Early Man in Charleston County two million years ago.' Rather, it appears that what you have found is the head of a Barbie doll, of the variety one of our staff, who has small children, believes to be the 'Malibu Barbie'. It is evident that you have given a great deal of thought to the analysis of this specimen, and you may be quite certain that those of us who are familiar with your prior work in the field were loath to come to contradiction with your findings. However, we do feel that there are a number of physical attributes of the specimen which might have tipped you off to its modern origin:

1. The material is molded plastic. Ancient hominid remains are typically fossilized bone.

2. The cranial capacity of the specimen is approximately 9 cubic centimeters, well below the threshold of even the earliest identified proto-hominids.

3. The dentition pattern evident on the 'skull' is more consistent with the common domesticated dog than it is with the 'ravenous man-eating Pliocene clams' you speculate roamed the wetlands during that time. This latter finding is certainly one of the most intriguing hypotheses you have submitted in your history with this institution, but the evidence seems to weigh rather heavily against it. Without going into too much detail, let us say that: A. The specimen looks like the head of a Barbie doll that a dog has chewed on. B. Clams don't have teeth.

It is with feelings tinged with melancholy that we must deny your request to have the specimen carbon dated. This is partially due to the heavy load our lab must bear in its normal operation, and partly due to carbon dating's notorious inaccuracy in fossils of recent geologic record. To the best of our knowledge, no Barbie dolls were produced prior to 1956 AD, and carbon dating is likely to produce wildly inaccurate results. Sadly, we must also deny your request that we approach the National Science Foundation's Phylogeny Department with the concept of assigning your specimen the scientific name 'Australopithecus spiff-arino.' Speaking personally, I, for one, fought tenaciously for the acceptance of your proposed taxonomy, but was ultimately voted down because the species name you selected was hyphenated, and didn't really sound like it might be Latin.

However, we gladly accept your generous donation of this fascinating specimen to the museum. While it is undoubtedly not a hominid fossil, it is, nonetheless, yet another riveting example of the great body of work you seem to accumulate here so effortlessly. You should know that our Director has reserved a special shelf in his own office for the display of the specimens you have previously submitted to the Institution, and the entire staff speculates daily on what you will happen upon next in your digs at the site you have discovered in your back yard. We eagerly anticipate your trip to our nation's capital that you proposed in your last letter, and several of us are pressing the Director to pay for it. We are particularly interested in hearing you expand on your theories surrounding the 'trans-positating fillifitation of ferrous ions in a structural matrix' that makes the excellent juvenile Tyrannosaurus rex femur you recently discovered take on the deceptive appearance of a rusty 9mm Sears Craftsman automotive crescent wrench.

Yours in Science,
Harvey Rowe
Curator, Antiquities

Questions

If life isn't about humanity, then tell me what it's all about, because I'd love to know. Money and power aren't what life is about. It can't be.
Orlando Bloom

Freddie Mercury, the lead singer of the rock group Queen, who died of AIDS at the end of 1991, wrote in one of his last songs on The Miracle album: 'Does anybody know what we are living for?'

Not long ago, a Christian minister found himself on Ann Robinson's show, *The Weakest Link*. As many of you will know, Ann Robinson is an absolute tyrant on this programme, giving people a really hard time, trying to expose the flaws in their knowledge. She really went for the minister. Her final attempt to unsettle him was:

'I suppose you believe in the gospel, don't you?'

'Yes.'

'Well, then. I challenge you to sing the gospel to me in two sentences.'

The minister immediately sang: 'Here's to you Mrs Robinson. Jesus loves you more than you will know.'

Quotes

Only two things are infinite, the universe and human stupidity, and I'm not sure about the former.
Albert Einstein

Astronomers say the universe is finite, which is a comforting thought for those people who can't remember where they leave things.

It is well to remember that the entire universe, with one trifling exception, is composed of others.
John Andrew Holmes

I'm astounded by people who want to 'know' the universe when it's hard enough to find your way around Chinatown.
Woody Allen

Bargain: Something you can't use at a price you can't resist.
Franklin P. Jones

The surest sign that intelligent life exists elsewhere in the universe is that it has never tried to contact us.
Calvin and Hobbes

And this is planet Earth— named after the Extremely Aggressive Really Thick Humanoids — we leave them well alone

My opinions may have changed, but not the fact that I am right.
Ashleigh Brilliant

I think that all right-thinking people in this country are sick and tired of being told that ordinary, decent people are fed up in this country with being sick and tired. I'm certainly not! But I'm sick and tired of being told that I am!
Monty Python

Sometimes I lie awake at night, and I ask, 'Where have I gone wrong?' Then a voice says to me, 'This is going to take more than one night.'
Charlie Brown

Sacred cows make the best hamburgers.
Mark Twain

When I told the people of Northern Ireland that I was an atheist, a woman in the audience stood up and said, 'Yes, but is it the God of the Catholics or the God of the Protestants in whom you don't believe?'
Quentin Crisp

Racism

In his autobiography, Mahatma Gandhi wrote that during his student days he read the Gospels seriously and considered converting to Christianity. He believed that in the teachings of Jesus he could find the solution to the caste system that was dividing the people of India. So one Sunday he decided to attend services at a nearby church and talk to the minister about becoming a Christian. When he entered the sanctuary, however, the usher refused to give him a seat and suggested that he worship with his own people. Gandhi left the church and never returned.

'If Christians have caste differences also,' he said, 'I might as well remain a Hindu.'

That usher's prejudice not only betrayed Jesus but also turned a person away from trusting him as Saviour.

Reason

> Man thinks, God laughs.
>
> *Jewish proverb*

Poor human reason, when it trusts in itself, substitutes the strangest absurdities for the highest divine concepts.

John Chrysostom

I do not feel obliged to believe that the same God who has endowed us with sense, reason, and intellect has intended us to forgo their use.

Galileo Galilei

Man is a rational animal. He can think up a reason for anything he wants to believe.

Anatole France

Reason is a faculty far larger than mere objective force. When either the political or the scientific discourse announces itself as the voice of reason, it is playing God, and should be spanked and stood in the corner.

Ursula K. Le Guin

When you are arguing against Him you are arguing against the very power that makes you able to argue at all.

C. S. Lewis

Reason is the greatest enemy that faith has; it never comes to the aid of spiritual things, but – more frequently than not – struggles against the divine Word, treating with contempt all that emanates from God.

Martin Luther

The supreme function of reason is to show man that some things are beyond reason.

Blaise Pascal

One can never do without straightforward common sense in matters great as well as small.

Margaret Thatcher

Two and two continue to make four, in spite of the whine of the amateur for three, or the cry of the critic for five.

James Whistle

Reality

Reality is what refuses to go away when I stop believing in it.
Philip Dick

Either you deal with what is the reality, or you can be sure that the reality is going to deal with you.

Alex Haley

We live in a fantasy world, a world of illusion. The great task in life is to find reality.
Iris Murdoch

I believe in looking reality straight in the eye and denying it.
Garrison Keillor

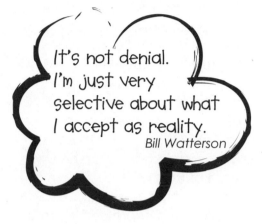

It's not denial. I'm just very selective about what I accept as reality.
Bill Watterson

Reality is something you rise above.
Liza Minnelli

Relativity

Relativity applies to physics, not ethics.
Albert Einstein

Repentance

The New Testament word for repentance means changing one's mind so that one's views, values, goals, and ways are changed and one's whole life is lived differently. The change is radical, both inwardly and outwardly; mind and judgment, will and affections, behavior and lifestyle, motives and purposes, are all involved. Repenting means starting a new life.
J. I. Packer

To my eternal shame, I even got my wife and daughter to back me up with witness statements supporting my lie. But then my opponents ambushed me in the middle of the trial with clear documentary evidence that I had told a lie on oath. My credibility as a witness was shattered. I had to withdraw from the libel case. And within 24 hours my whole life was shattered too. The former Cabinet Minister had impaled himself on his own sword of truth, with explosive and apocalyptic consequences. Some people have expressed surprise that I am still in one piece after being so torn to shreds in the onslaught of media vilification and castigation I received at the height of my dramas. A great deal of the criticism of me was vitriolic; some of it was vicious; and I deserved most of it. When these thunderbolts were raining in on me from all directions, I turned to my Christian faith, imperfect though it was, and began to ponder more deeply than ever before on the great themes in the gospels of love, penitence, redemption and resurrection. Although I am sceptical of fox-hole conversion, nevertheless the time when I was at the nadir of my misfortunes was the time when I turned more humbly and penitently than ever towards Our Lord Jesus Christ.

Jonathan Aitken (1999)

■ ■ ■ ■ ■ ■ ■ ■ ■ ■ ■ ■ ■ ■ ■ ■ ■ ■

A dead end street is a good place to turn around.

Naomi Judd

A Christian is a person who has the possibility of innumerable new starts.

Francis Schaeffer

You can't keep blaming yourself, Marge. Just blame yourself once and move on.

Homer Simpson

Everybody, soon or late, sits down to a banquet of consequences.

Robert Louis Stevenson

Safety

How to stay safe in the world today

- Avoid riding in cars, because they are responsible for 20% of all fatal accidents.
- Do not stay at home, because 17% of all accidents occur in the home.
- Avoid walking on streets or sidewalks, because 14% of all accidents happen to pedestrians.
- Avoid travelling by air, rail or water, because 16% of all accidents involve these forms of transport.
- Of the remaining 33%, 32% of all deaths occur in hospitals. So, above all else, *avoid hospitals*.

But, you will be pleased to learn that only 0.001% of all deaths occur in worship services in church, and these are usually related to previous physical disorders. Therefore, logic tells us that the *safest* place for you to be at any given point in time is at church!

And Bible study is safe too. The percentage of deaths during Bible study is even less.

So, attend church, and read your Bible. *It could save your life!*

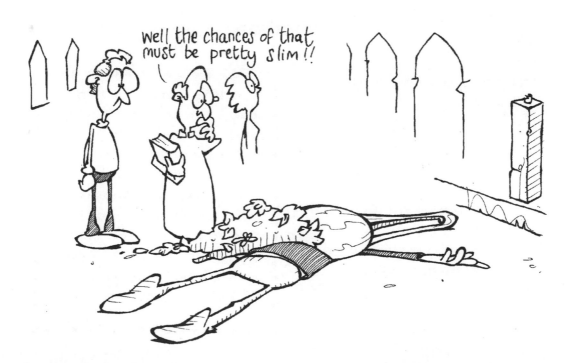

Salvation

A guy walking in the desert desperately needed a drink. As he followed the dunes, he came upon another man riding a camel. He asked the man if he had something to drink.

The man on the camel said, 'No, but if you like, I have a nice selection of ties. Would you like to buy one?'

'No!' the first man replied. 'Are you crazy? I need something to drink, not a tie!'

So the man on the camel rode on, and the walking man continued his slow and very thirsty trek for several days. Finally he came upon a cantina.
He gratefully approached the doorman at the cantina and said, 'I'm so glad I made it! Can I get in and get some water?'

The doorman frowned at him. 'Not without a tie.'

Samaritan

Attitudes displayed in the Parable of the Good Samaritan:

- *The Robbers:* What's yours is mine if I can get it.
- *The Priest:* What's mine is mine if I can keep it.
- *The Innkeeper:* What's mine is yours if you can pay for it.
- *The Samaritan:* What's mine is yours if you need it.

Tear Fund

An elderly man was beaten badly by thugs and left lying in the gutter and in pain. The first passer-by averted his gaze; the second did the same. Nobody wanted to know until a social worker on her way home came to the spot. She looked down at the recumbent figure and said, 'Tut, tut! Whoever did this needs help!'

Sayings

If you can't be kind, at least have the decency to be vague.

If you can keep your head, while all around you are losing theirs – then you probably haven't understood the seriousness of the situation.

The years have been kind to us, but gravity isn't doing us any favours.

You can give without loving but you cannot love without giving.

The Second Coming

I wish he [Jesus] would come in my lifetime so that I could take off my crown and lay it at his feet.

Queen Victoria

Service

If you are not involved in any service or ministry, what excuse have you been using? Abraham was old, Jacob was insecure, Leah was unattractive, Joseph was abused, Moses stuttered, Gideon was poor, Samson was co-dependent, Rahab was immoral, David had an affair and all kinds of family problems, Elijah was suicidal, Jeremiah was depressed, Jonah was reluctant, Naomi was a widow, John the Baptist was eccentric to say the least, Peter was impulsive and hot–tempered, Martha worried a lot, the Samaritan woman had several failed marriages, Zacchaeus was unpopular, Thomas had doubts, Paul had poor health, and Timothy was timid. That's quite a variety of misfits, but God used each of them in his service. He will use you, too, if you stop making excuses.

Rick Warren

Dear Pastor:

There are 566 members in our church, but 100 are frail and elderly. That leaves 466 to do all the work.

However, 80 are young people away at college. That leaves 386 to do all the work.

However, 150 of them are tired businessmen, so that leaves 236 to do all the work.

150 are housewives with children. That leaves 86 to do all the work.

There are also 46 members who have other important interests. Which leaves 40 to do all the work, but 15 live too far away to come regularly. So that leaves 25 to do all the work.

And 23 of them say they've done their part. So, Pastor, that leaves *you* and *me* and, frankly, I'm exhausted.

Good luck to you.

A. Parishioner

Everybody can be great...because anybody can serve. You don't have to have a college degree to serve. You don't have to make your subject and verb agree to serve. You only need a heart full of grace. A soul generated by love.

Dr Martin Luther King Jr

Once survival has become our supreme goal, we have lost our way... the church is not called to survive history but to serve humanity. As with each individual, there is a difference between living and existing for the church... The church exists to serve as the body of Christ, and it is through this commitment to serve that we are forced to engage our culture... The serving that we are called to requires direct contact. You cannot wash the feet of a dirty world if you refuse to touch it.

Erwin Mc Manus

You may be familiar with Albrecht Dürer's famous painting *The Praying Hands*, but do you know the story behind it? The painting was inspired by the sacrificial, loving acts of a friend.

Dürer and an older friend were struggling to make a go of it as artists. Recognizing Dürer's talent, the older man took a job to provide for both of them until Dürer could complete his art studies. The work was labour, but he did it gladly for his friend.

Finally, Dürer made a sale. The money was enough to care for both of them for several months. Now his older friend could resume his painting, but the older man's hands had become so stiff from the hard labour that he was unable to paint.

One day when Dürer returned home, he found his friend in prayer, his work-worn hands folded reverently. Dürer painted a picture of these hands, capturing them for ages to come as a memorial to the love and sacrifice of his older friend.

Significance

Significance is the attainment of noble goals for the sake of others rather than at their expense.

J. Ryle

Signs

Four rabbis had a series of theological arguments, and three were always in accord against the fourth. One day, the odd rabbi out, after the usual '3-to-1, majority rules' statement that signified that he had lost again, decided to appeal to a higher authority.

'Oh, God!' he cried. 'I know in my heart that I am right and they are wrong! Please give me a sign to prove it to them!'

It was a beautiful, sunny day. As soon as the rabbi finished his prayer, a stormcloud moved across the sky above the four. It rumbled once and dissolved.

'A sign from God! See, I'm right, I knew it!'

But the other three disagreed, pointing out that stormclouds form on hot days.

So the rabbi prayed again: 'Oh, God, I need a bigger sign to show that I am right and they are wrong. So please, God, a bigger sign!'

This time four stormclouds appeared, rushed toward each other to form one big cloud, and a bolt of lightning slammed into a tree on a nearby hill.

'I told you I was right!' cried the rabbi, but his friends insisted that nothing had happened that could not be explained by natural causes.

The rabbi was getting ready to ask for a very big sign, but just as he said, 'Oh God…,' the sky turned pitch black, the earth shook, and a deep, booming voice intoned, *'Heeeeeeee's riiiiiight!'*

The rabbi put his hands on his hips, turned to the other three, and said, 'Well?'

'So,' shrugged one of the other rabbis, 'now it's 3 to 2.'

Signs (outside churches)

- Give God what's right – not what's left.
- Man's way leads to a hopeless end! God's way leads to an endless hope.
- A lot of kneeling will keep you in good standing.
- Don't wait for six strong men to take you to church.
- The church is prayer-conditioned.
- Suffering from truth decay? Brush up on your Bible.
- Exercise daily – walk with the Lord.
- Give Satan an inch and he'll be a ruler.

Sin

Global recall notice

The Maker of all human beings is recalling all units manufactured, regardless of make or year, due to a serious defect in the primary and central component of the heart.

This is due to a malfunction in the original prototype units code named Adam and Eve, resulting in the reproduction of the same defect in all subsequent units.

This defect has been technically termed 'Subsequential Internal Non-morality', or more commonly known as SIN, as it is primarily expressed.

Symptoms include:

- Loss of direction
- Foul vocal emissions
- Amnesia of origin
- Lack of peace and joy
- Selfish or violent behaviour
- Depression or confusion in the mental component
- Fearfulness
- Idolatry
- Rebellion

The Manufacturer, who is neither liable nor at fault for this defect, is providing factory-authorized repair and service free of charge to correct this SIN defect. The Repair Technician, Jesus, has most generously offered to bear the entire burden of the staggering cost of these repairs. There is no additional fee required.

The number to call for repair in all areas is P-R-A-Y-E-R.

Once connected, please upload your burden of SIN through the REPENTANCE procedure. Next, download REMISSION from the Repair Technician, Jesus, into the heart component. No matter how big or small the SIN defect is, Jesus will replace it with:

- Love
- Joy
- Peace
- Patience
- Kindness
- Goodness
- Faithfulness
- Gentleness
- Self-control

Please see the operating manual, the B.I.B.L.E. (Basic Instructions Before Leaving Earth), for further details on the use of these fixes.

WARNING: Continuing to operate the human being unit without correction voids any manufacturer warranties, exposing the unit to dangers and problems too numerous to list and will result in the human unit being permanently impounded.

DANGER: The human being units not responding to this recall action will need to be scrapped in the furnace. The SIN defect will not be permitted to enter Heaven, so as to prevent contamination of that facility.

Thank you for your attention!

GOD

Please assist where possible by notifying others of this important recall notice, and you may contact the Father any time by 'kneemail'.

There is a common English word that is nine letters long. Each time you remove a letter from it, it still remains an English word – from nine letters right down to a single letter.

What is the original word, and what are the words that it becomes after removing one letter at a time?

The word is startling – starting – staring – string – sting – sing – sin – in – I.

A Sunday School teacher asked her class, 'Does anyone here know what we mean by "sins of omission"?'

A small girl replied, 'Aren't those the sins we should have committed, but didn't?'

Slogans

Actual T-shirt slogans

- Frankly, Scallop, I don't give a Clam. *(Seen on Cape Cod.)*
- That's it! I'm calling Grandma! *(Seen on an eight-year-old.)*
- Wrinkled was not one of the things I wanted to be when I grew up.
- Procrastinate now.
- Rehab is for quitters.
- I have a degree in Liberal Arts! Do you want fries with that?
- Finally 21 & legally able to do everything I've been doing since 15.
- All men are idiots, and I married their king!
- West Virginia: 1 million people, 15 last names.
- I'm out of oestrogen and I've got a gun!
- A hangover is the wrath of grapes.
- A journey of a thousand miles begins with a cash advance.
- Stupidity is not a handicap. Park elsewhere!
- Discourage inbreeding – ban Country Music.
- He who dies with the most toys is still dead.
- Heck is where people go who don't believe in gosh.
- One picture is worth a thousand words, but it uses up a thousand times more memory.
- The meek shall inherit the earth… after we're through with it.
- Time flies like an arrow. Fruit flies like a banana.
- Ham & Eggs – a day's work for a chicken; a life commitment for a pig.
- Welcome to Kentucky – set your watch back 20 years.
- The trouble with life is there's no background music.
- Suicidal twin kills sister by mistake!
- The original point-and-click interface was a Smith & Wesson.
- My wild oats have turned to shredded wheat.
- Computer programmers don't byte, they just nibble a bit.
- Mop & Glow – the floor wax used by the Three Mile Island clean-up team.
- Nyquil – the stuffy, sneezy, why-is-this-room-spinning medicine.
- Quoting one is plagiarism. Quoting many is research.
- My husband and I divorced over religious differences. He thought he was God and I didn't.

Slogans for women's T-shirts

- So many men, so few can afford me.
- God made us sisters; Prozac made us friends.
- If they don't have chocolate in heaven, I ain't going.
- At my age, I've seen it all, done it all, heard it all... I just can't remember it all.
- My mother is a travel agent for guilt trips.
- Princess, having had sufficient experience with Princes, seeks frog.
- Coffee, chocolate, men...some things are just better rich.
- Don't treat me any differently than you would the Queen.
- If you want breakfast in bed, sleep in the kitchen.
- Dinner is ready when the smoke alarm goes off.
- It's hard to be nostalgic when you can't remember anything.
- Guys have feelings too. But, like... who cares?
- Next mood swing: 6 minutes.
- I hate everybody...and you're next.
- And your point is...?
- I used to be a schizophrenic, but we're OK now.
- Warning: I have an attitude and I know how to use it.
- Do not start with me. You will not win.
- You have the right to remain silent, so please shut up.
- All stressed out and no one to choke.
- I'm one of those bad things that happen to good people.
- How can I miss you if you won't go away?
- Sorry if I look interested. I'm not.
- If we are what we eat, I'm fast, cheap and easy.
- Don't upset me! I'm running out of places to hide the bodies.

Some random thoughts for those who take life too seriously

- Save the whales. Collect the whole set.
- A day without sunshine is like, night.
- On the other hand, you have different fingers.
- I just got lost in thought. It was unfamiliar territory.
- 42.7 per cent of all statistics are made up on the spot.
- 99 per cent of lawyers give the rest a bad name.
- I feel like I'm diagonally parked in a parallel universe.
- You have the right to remain silent. Anything you say will be

- misquoted, then used against you.
- I wonder how much deeper the ocean would be without sponges.
- Honk if you love peace and quiet.
- Remember, half the people you know are below average.
- Despite the cost of living, have you noticed how popular it remains?
- Nothing is foolproof to a talented fool.
- Atheism is a non-prophet organization.
- He who laughs last thinks slowest.
- Depression is merely anger without enthusiasm.
- Eagles may soar, but weasels don't get sucked into jet engines.
- The early bird may get the worm, but the second mouse gets the cheese.
- I drive way too fast to worry about cholesterol.
- I intend to live forever – so far so good.
- Borrow money from a pessimist – they don't expect it back.
- If Barbie is so popular, why do you have to buy her friends?
- My mind is like a steel trap – rusty and illegal in 37 states.
- Quantum mechanics: The dreams stuff is made of.
- The only substitute for good manners is fast reflexes.

Smartness

None of us is as
smart as all of us.
Ken Blanchard

Stars/superstition

44% of women 'believe in ghosts' compared with 31% of men. Twice as many women as men read horoscopes (31% to 14%). 22% of women 'believe in heaven but not hell' compared with just 9% of men. 50% of women and 26% of men believe in guardian angels.

The Guardian

Stress

An honest man is being tailgated by a stressed-out woman on a busy boulevard. Suddenly, the light turns yellow, just in front of him. He does the honest thing, and stops at the crosswalk, even though he could have beaten the red light by accelerating through the intersection. The tailgating woman hits the roof and honks her horn, screaming in frustration as she misses her chance to get through the intersection with him.

As she is still in mid-rant, she hears a tap on her window and looks up into the face of a very serious police officer. The officer orders her to exit her car with her hands up. He takes her to the police station where she is searched, fingerprinted, photographed, and placed in a cell.

After a couple of hours, a policeman approaches the cell and opens the door. She is escorted back to the booking desk where the arresting officer is waiting with her personal effects. He says, 'I'm very sorry for this mistake. You see, I pulled up behind your car while you were blowing your horn, flipping the guy off in front of you, and cussing a blue streak at him. I noticed the "Choose Life" licence-plate holder, the "What Would Jesus Do" bumper sticker, the "Follow Me to Sunday School" bumper sticker, and the chrome-plated Christian fish emblem on the trunk. So, naturally, I assumed you had stolen the car.'

Stupidity

The seven most stupid people of 2004

1. I am a medical student currently doing a rotation in toxicology at the poison control centre. Today, this woman called in very upset because she caught her little daughter eating ants. I quickly reassured her that the ants are not harmful and there would be no need to bring her daughter into the hospital. She calmed down and at the end of the conversation happened to mention that she gave her daughter some ant poison to eat in order to kill the ants. I told her that she'd better bring her daughter into the emergency room right away.

2. Early this year, some Boeing employees on the airfield decided to steal a life raft from one of the 747s. They were successful in getting it out of the plane and home. Shortly after they took it for a float on the river, they noticed a Coast Guard helicopter coming towards them. It turned out that the chopper was homing in on the emergency locator beacon that activated when the raft was inflated. They are no longer employed at Boeing.

3. A true story out of San Francisco: A man, wanting to rob a downtown Bank of America, walked into the branch and wrote 'This iz a stikkup. Put all your muny in this bag.' While standing in line, waiting to give his note to the teller, he began to worry that someone had seen him write the note and might call the police before he reached the teller's window. So he left the Bank of America and crossed the street to Wells Fargo. After waiting a few minutes in line, he handed his note to the Wells Fargo teller. She read it and, surmising from his spelling errors that he wasn't the brightest light in the harbour, told him that she could not accept his stickup note because it was written on a Bank of America deposit slip and that he would either have to fill out a Wells Fargo deposit slip or go back to Bank of America.

Looking somewhat defeated, the man said, 'OK' and left. He was arrested a few minutes later, as he was waiting in line back at the Bank of America.

4. A guy walked into a little corner store with a shotgun and demanded all of the cash from the cash drawer. After the cashier put the cash in a bag, the robber

saw a bottle of scotch that he wanted behind the counter on the shelf. He told the cashier to put it in the bag as well, but the cashier refused and said, 'Because I don't believe you are over twenty-one.' The robber said he was, but the clerk still refused to give it to him because he didn't believe him. At that point, the robber took his driver's licence out of his wallet and gave it to the clerk. The clerk looked it over and agreed that the man was in fact over twenty-one and he put the scotch in the bag.

The robber then ran from the store with his loot. The cashier promptly called the police and gave the name and address of the robber that he got off the licence. They arrested the robber two hours later.

5. A pair of Michigan robbers entered a record shop nervously waving revolvers. The first one shouted, 'Nobody move!' When his partner moved, the startled first bandit shot him.

6. Seems this guy wanted some beer pretty badly. He decided that he'd just throw a cinder block through a liquor store window, grab some booze, and run. So he lifted the cinder block and heaved it over his head at the window. The cinder block bounced back and hit the would-be thief on the head, knocking him unconscious. It seems the liquor store window was made of Plexiglas. The whole event was caught on videotape. Oh, that hurts!

7. The *Ann Arbor News* crime column reported that a man walked into a Burger King in Ypsilanti, Michigan at 12:50 a.m., flashed a gun and demanded cash. The clerk turned him down because he said he couldn't open the cash register without a food order. When the man ordered onion rings, the clerk said they weren't available for breakfast. The man, frustrated, walked away.

Synergy

Did you know that one horse can pull two tons whereas two horses can pull twenty-seven tons? When churches work together we definitely see a multiplication.

Suffering

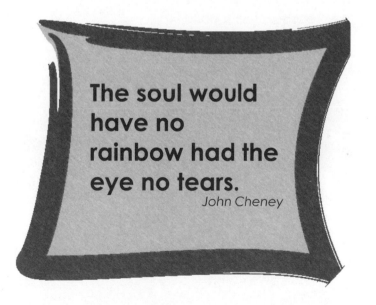

The soul would have no rainbow had the eye no tears.
John Cheney

Teachers

The children had all been photographed, and the teacher was trying to persuade them each to buy a copy of the group picture.

'Just think how nice it will be to look at it when you are all grown up and say, "There's Jennifer, she's a lawyer," or "That's Michael, he's a doctor."'

A small voice at the back of the room rang out, 'And there's the teacher, she's dead.'

A teacher was giving a lesson on the circulation of the blood. Trying to make the matter clearer, she said, 'Now, class, if I stood on my head, the blood, as you know, would run into it, and I would turn red in the face.'

'Yes,' the class said.

'Then why is it that while I am standing upright in the ordinary position the blood doesn't run into my feet?'

A little fellow shouted, ''Cause your feet ain't empty.'

Thanksgiving

An elderly man in Florida calls his son in New York. The father says to the son, 'I hate to tell you, but we've got some troubles here in the house. Your mother and I can't stand each other any more, and we're getting a divorce. I've had it! I want to live out the rest of my years in peace. I'm telling you now, so you and your sister won't go into shock later when I move out.'

He hangs up, and the son immediately calls his sister in the Hamptons and tells her the news. The sister says, 'I'll handle this!' She calls Florida and says to her father, 'Don't do *anything* until we get there! We'll be there Wednesday night.'

The father agrees. He hangs up the phone and hollers to his wife, 'OK, they're coming for Thanksgiving. Now, what are we going to tell them for Christmas?'

A young man named John received a parrot as a gift. The parrot had a bad attitude and an even worse vocabulary. Every word out of the bird's mouth was rude, obnoxious and laced with profanity.

John tried and tried to change the bird's attitude by consistently saying only polite words, playing soft music and anything else he could think of to 'clean up' the bird's vocabulary. Finally, John was fed up and he yelled at the parrot.

The parrot yelled back. John shook the parrot and the parrot got angrier and even ruder. John, in desperation, threw up his hand, grabbed the bird and put him in the freezer. For a few minutes the parrot squawked and kicked and screamed. Then suddenly there was total quiet. Not a peep was heard for over a minute. Fearing that he'd hurt the parrot, John quickly opened the door to the freezer.

The parrot calmly stepped out onto John's outstretched arms and said, 'I believe I may have offended you with my rude language and actions. I'm sincerely remorseful for my inappropriate transgressions and I fully intend to do everything I can to correct my rude and unforgivable behaviour.'

John was stunned at the change in the bird's attitude. As he was about to ask the parrot what had made such a dramatic change in his behaviour, the bird continued:

'May I ask what the turkey did?'

Happy Thanksgiving!

What are you thankful for today?

1. WAKE UP!

Decide to have a good day. 'This is the day the Lord hath made; let us rejoice and be glad in it' (Psalm 118:24).

2. DRESS UP!

The best way to dress up is to put on a smile. A smile is an inexpensive way to improve your looks. 'The Lord does not look at the things man looks at. Man looks at the outward appearance, but the Lord looks at the heart' (1 Samuel 16:7).

3. SHUT UP!

Say nice things and learn to listen. God gave us two ears and one mouth, so he must have meant for us to do twice as much listening as talking. 'He who guards his lips guards his soul' (Proverbs 13:3).

4. STAND UP!...

for what you believe in. Stand for something or you will fall for anything. 'Let us not be weary in doing good; for at the proper time, we will reap a harvest if we do not give up. Therefore, as we have opportunity, let us do good' (Galatians 6:9–10).

5. LOOK UP!...

to the Lord. 'I can do everything through Christ who strengthens me' (Philippians 4:13).

6. REACH UP!...

for something higher. 'Trust in the Lord with all your heart, and lean not unto your own understanding. In all your ways, acknowledge him, and he will direct your path' (Proverbs 3:5–6).

7. LIFT UP!...

your prayers. 'Do not worry about anything; instead *pray about everything*' (Philippians 4:6).

Time

We spend our lives on the run: we get up by the clock, eat and sleep by the clock, get up again, go to work – and then we retire. And what do they give us? A clock.

Dave Allen

Today is the first day of the rest of your life – but so was yesterday and look how you messed that up!

The last ten minutes

What would you do right now if you learned that you were going to die in ten minutes?... It's hard to say, but of all the things you might do in your final ten minutes, it's a pretty safe bet that few of them are things you actually did today. Now, some people will bemoan this fact, wag their fingers in your direction, and tell you sternly that you should live every minute of your life as though it were your last, which only goes to show that some people would spend their final ten minutes giving other people dumb advice.

Daniel Gilbert,
Stumbling Upon Happiness

Slow dance

Have you ever watched kids on a
merry-go-round?
Or listened to the rain
Slapping on the ground?

Ever followed a butterfly's erratic
flight?
Or gazed at the sun into the
fading night?

You'd better slow down.
Don't dance so fast.
Time is short.
The music won't last.

Do you run through each day
On the fly?
When you ask, 'How are you?'
Do you hear the reply?

When the day is done
Do you lie in your bed
With the next hundred chores
Running through your head?

You'd better slow down.
Don't dance so fast.
Time is short.
The music won't last.

Ever told your child,
'We'll do it tomorrow'?
And in your haste,
Not seen his sorrow?

Ever lost touch,
Let a good friendship die
'Cause you never had time
To call and say, 'Hi'?

You'd better slow down.
Don't dance so fast.
Time is short.
The music won't last.

When you run so fast to get
somewhere
You miss half the fun of getting
there.
When you worry and hurry
through your day,
It is like an unopened gift...
Thrown away.

Life is not a race.
Do take it slower.
Hear the music
Before the song is over.

*Written by a terminally ill girl in
a New York hospital*

It had been some time since Jack had seen the old man. In fact, Jack moved across the country in pursuit of his dreams. In the rush of his busy life, Jack had little time to think about the past and often no time to spend with his wife and son. He was working on his future, and nothing could stop him.

Over the phone, his mother told him, 'Mr Belser died last night. The funeral is Wednesday.' Memories flashed through his mind like an old newsreel as he sat quietly remembering his childhood days. 'Jack, did you hear me?'

'Oh, sorry, Mum. Yes, I heard you. It's been so long since I thought of him. I'm sorry, but I honestly thought he died years ago,' Jack said.

'Well, he didn't forget you. Every time I saw him he'd ask how you were doing. He'd reminisce about the many days you spent over "his side of the fence", as he put it,' Mum told him.

'I loved that old house he lived in,' Jack said.

'You know, Jack, after your father died, Mr Belser stepped in to make sure you had a man's influence in your life,' she said.

'He's the one who taught me carpentry,' he said. 'I wouldn't be in this business if it weren't for him. He spent a lot of time teaching me things he thought were important… Mum, I'll be there for the funeral,' Jack said.

As busy as he was, he kept his word. Jack caught the next flight to his hometown. Mr Belser's funeral was small and uneventful. He had no children of his own, and most of his relatives had passed away.

The night before he had to return home, Jack and his Mum stopped by to see the old house next door one more time. Standing in the doorway, Jack paused for a moment. It was like crossing over into another dimension, a leap through space and time. The house was exactly as he remembered. Every step held memories. Every picture, every piece of furniture… Jack stopped suddenly.

'What's wrong, Jack?' his Mum asked.

'The box is gone,' he said.

'What box?' Mum asked.

'There was a small gold box that he kept locked on top of his desk. I must have asked him a thousand times what was inside. All he'd ever tell me was, "The thing I value most."'

It was gone. Everything about the house was exactly how Jack remembered it, except for the box. He figured someone from the Belser family had taken it. 'Now I'll never know what was so valuable to him,' Jack said.

'I'd better get some sleep. I have an early flight home, Mum.'

It had been about two weeks since Mr Belser died. Returning home from work one day, Jack discovered a note in his mailbox. 'Signature required on a package. No one at home. Please stop by the main post office within the next three days,' the note read.

Early the next day Jack retrieved the package. The small box was old and looked like it had been mailed a hundred years ago. The handwriting was difficult to read, but the return address caught his attention. 'Mr Harold Belser', it read. Jack took the box out to his car and ripped open the package. There inside was the gold box and an envelope. Jack's hands shook as he read the note inside:

> 'Upon my death, please forward this box and its contents to Jack Bennett. It's the thing I valued most in my life.'

A small key was taped to the letter. His heart racing, tears filling his eyes, Jack carefully unlocked the box. There inside he found a beautiful gold pocket watch. Running his fingers slowly over the finely etched casing, he unlatched the cover. Inside he found these words engraved: 'Jack, thanks for your time! –Harold Belser.'

'The thing he valued most...was... my time,' Jack said to himself.

Titles

The first children's book published in America was written by the Puritan preacher John Cotton and printed in Cambridge, Massachusetts, in 1646. Its title was *Spiritual Milk for Boston Babes in Either England Drawn from the Breasts of Both Testaments for Their Souls' Nourishment*.

Some imaginary book titles

- *Full Assurance* by May B. Knot
- *The Protestant Work Ethic* by Daly Grind
- *Pray Continually* by Neil A. Lot
- *Salt of the Earth* by Pastor Pepper
- *Intercession* by Frank and Ernest Pleading
- *Praise in the USA* by Hal E. Looyah

Some real but strange book titles

- *The Joy of Chickens*
- *American Bottom Archeology*
- *Versailles: The View From Sweden*
- *Re-using Old Graves*
- *Highlights in the History of Concrete*
- *Greek Rural Postmen and Their Cancellation Numbers*
- *People Who Don't Know They're Dead: How They Attach Themselves to Unsuspecting Bystanders and What to Do About It*
- *The Stray Shopping Carts of Eastern North America: A Guide to Field Identification*

From BBC News

Tortillas

In 1950 tortilla production at the El Zarape Tortilla Factory in Los Angeles was automated. The factory could now churn out twelve times more tortillas than anyone could by hand. But the machine also had its setbacks – many of the tortillas came out misshapen and had to be thrown away. But a line worker called Rebecca Carranza saw something in the rejects that fascinated her. She began saving the discarded tortillas, cut them into triangles and fried them. Trying them out at a family party, they were an instant success. In fact, Mrs Carranza went on to eventually run the company, and created the famous 'tortilla chips' that fill supermarket shelves world-wide.

Rebecca Carranza died at 98 years old, still considered the inventor of the tortilla chip. She wasn't educated, rich or well connected, but she had vision – the kind of vision we need to take what is rejected and discarded and, by the grace of God, put life into it.

Triviality

Don't let the littleness in others bring out the littleness in you.
Seen on a church marquee

Truth

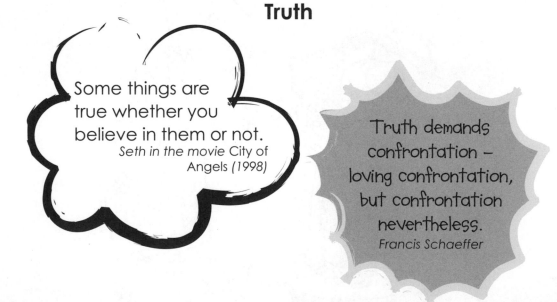

Some things are true whether you believe in them or not.
Seth in the movie City of Angels *(1998)*

Truth demands confrontation – loving confrontation, but confrontation nevertheless.
Francis Schaeffer

Uniqueness

We all know we are unique individuals, but we tend to see others as representatives of groups.

Deborah Tanne

There is repetition everywhere, and nothing is found only once in the world.

Goethe

Unity

Among the unsaved people on earth, what is the prevailing image of Christians today? It's not the dedicated and inspired work of our missionaries. It's not the great preaching of Billy Graham or others who inspire people. It's the image of divisions among brothers and sisters in Christ as we struggle for authority or argue about the interpretation of individual verses in the Holy Scriptures.

Jimmy Carter

Unity in things Necessary, Liberty in things Unnecessary, and Charity in all.

Richard Baxter (1651)

I may worship in a different building from you, I may worship in a different style, but all we hold dear is God's gift in Christ Jesus, who is our Unity. In Him we have all and lack nothing.

Michael J. Davis

When we talk about what we believe we divide. When we talk about who we believe in we unite.

E. Stanley Jones

Unity is the ultimate goal of all the ways of God.

Abraham Kuyper

Urgency

Let's live as though Christ died yesterday, rose from the dead today and is coming back tomorrow with joy, hope, passion, and urgency.

Simon Griellband

Valentines

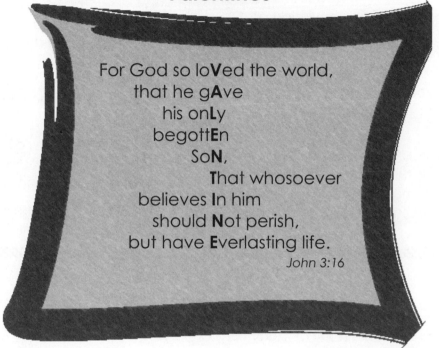

For God so lo**V**ed the world,
that he g**A**ve
his on**L**y
begott**E**n
So**N**,
That whosoever
believes **I**n him
should **N**ot perish,
but have **E**verlasting life.

John 3:16

Vicars

The vicar was lying in hospital, recovering from an operation, when the churchwarden came to visit.

'How was the Church Council meeting last night?' asked the vicar.

'Well,' said the warden, 'the good news is that we passed a vote wishing you a full and quick recovery.'

'Oh, that's nice. What's the bad news?'

'It was passed by 14 votes to 12.'

The minister of a Baptist church decided that God was calling the church to a new vision of what it should be and do. So at the Elders' Meeting, he presented the new vision with as much energy, conviction and passion as he could muster. When he had finished and sat down, the chairman of the meeting called for a vote. All fourteen elders voted against the new vision, with only the minister voting for it.

'Well, pastor, it looks like you will have to think again,' said the chairman. 'Would you like to close the meeting in prayer?'

So the minister stood up, raised his hand to heaven, and prayed, 'Lord, will you not show these people that this is not *my* vision but *your* vision!'

At that moment, the clouds darkened, thunder rolled, and a streak of lightning burst through the window and struck in two the table at which they were sitting, throwing the minister and all the elders to the ground.

After a moment's silence, as they all got up and dusted themselves off, the chairman spoke again.

'Well, that's fourteen votes to two, then.'

Vision

In an amazing longitudinal study on goal setting, Yale University surveyed the graduating class of 1953 on commencement day, to determine if they had written goals for what they wanted their lives to become. Only 3 per cent had such a vision. In 1973, the surviving members of the class of 1953 were surveyed again. The 3 per cent who had a vision for what they wished their lives to become had accumulated greater wealth than the other 97 per cent combined.

Vulnerability

- The probability of being killed by a terrorist is 1 in 420,000.
- The probability of being killed by accident (mostly on the road) is 1 in 30.
- The probability of being killed in a British mother's womb is 1 in 5.

Walks

I like long walks, especially when taken by people who annoy me.
Noel Coward

Weaknesses

This is what a selection committee would have said about the Old Testament heroes, had they applied for the post of a parish Vicar:

- *Noah:* prone to unrealistic building projects; he was Vicar of his former parish for 120 years and didn't have one single person converted.
- *Joseph:* a big thinker but also a big head; a bit OTT on the Dream Interpretation front and has a prison record.
- *Moses:* a modest and meek man but a poor communicator who even stutters at times. Sometimes he blows his top and smashes rocks. There is also a rumour he had to leave a previous job because of a murder rap.

- *David:* the most promising candidate of all until we discovered the affair he had with his neighbour's wife.
- *Solomon:* Great preacher, but how are we going to fit 700 wives into the Vicarage?

- *Jeremiah:* emotionally unstable, alarmist, negative, always lamenting things and bursting into tears, and was also said to have taken a long trip to bury his underwear on the bank of a foreign river.

- *John:* says he is a Baptist, so that rules him out. Also, he doesn't dress very well and sleeps outdoors for months on end. He has a weird diet and provokes Bishops and Archdeacons...

And that, of course, would never do!

Weather

Q. What do you call two straight days of rain in Britain?

A. A weekend.

> Two Viking invaders are trudging up the beach in the pouring rain. One looks skywards and says, 'So this is England. What's it like?'
>
> The other snarls, 'Well, if you like the weather, you'll love the food.'

You're hiking around on Hampstead Heath at the end of a long sunny day. You run across (separately) the ghosts of Sir Winston Churchill, Sir Baden Powell and Sir Edmund Hillary, who all give you directions to the nearest tube stop.

Whom don't you believe?

Your storyteller, for there is no such thing as a completely sunny day in England.

It only rains twice a year in Britain: August to April and May to July.

The USA has only three hurricane warning centres – Coral Gables, FL, Guam, and Honolulu, HI (recently completed). All three have faced Category 4 hurricanes in the past month. Which only goes to show: If you build it, they will come!

A newcomer to Britain arrives on a rainy day. He gets up the next day and it's raining. It also rains the day after that, and the day after that.

He goes out to lunch and sees a young kid and asks in despair, 'Hey kid, does it ever stop raining around here?'

The kid says, 'How do I know? I'm only six.'

Q. What's the definition of a British optimist?

A. A guy with a sun-visor on his rain-hat.

Funny exam answers on weather

- The tides are a fight between the earth and the moon. All water tends towards the moon, because there is no water in the moon, and nature abhors a vacuum. I forget where the sun joins in this fight.
- Dew is formed on leaves when the sun shines down on them and makes them perspire.
- I am not sure how clouds get formed. But the clouds know how to do it, and that is the important thing.
- Most books now say our sun is a star. But it still knows how to change back into a sun in the daytime.
- Some people can tell what time it is by looking at the sun. But I have never been able to make out the numbers.
- Rain is saved up in cloud banks.
- Thunder is a rich source of loudness.
- Isotherms and isobars are even more important than their names sound.
- Clouds are high-flying fogs.

All kinds of weather remarks

- The wind is like the air, only pushier.
- You can listen to thunder after lightning and tell how close you came to getting hit. If you don't hear it you got hit, so never mind.
- Climate is what you expect. Weather is what you get!
- Don't knock the weather; nine out of ten people couldn't start a conversation if it didn't change once in a while.
- I had just moved north and was feeling apprehensive about the severity of the winters in my new home. My anxious queries about the weather brought this reply from a native: 'Ma'am, we have four seasons here: early winter, midwinter, late winter and next winter.'

Out in Kansas, tornadoes often hit with sudden devastation, and without warning. In one case, a house was completely whisked away, leaving only the foundation and first floor. A silver-haired farm lady was seen sitting dazed, in a bathtub, the only remaining part of the house left above the floor. The rescue squad rushed to her aid and found her unhurt.

She was just sitting there in the tub, talking to herself. 'It was the most amazing thing...it was the most amazing thing,' she kept repeating dazedly.

'What was the most amazing thing, Ma'am?' asked one of the rescuers.

'I was visiting my daughter here, taking a bath, and all I did was pull the plug, and dog-gone-it if the whole house didn't suddenly drain away!'

The Michaels family owned a small farm in Canada, just yards away from the North Dakota border. Their land had been the subject of a minor dispute between the United States and Canada for generations. Mrs Michaels, who had just celebrated her ninetieth birthday, lived on the farm with her son and three grandchildren.

One day, her son came into her room holding a letter. 'I just got some news, Mum,' he said. 'The government has come to an agreement with the people in Washington. They've decided that our land is really part of the United States. We have the right to approve or disapprove of the agreement. What do you think?'

'What do I think?' his mother said. 'Jump at it! Call them right now and tell them we accept! I don't think I could stand another one of those Canadian winters!'

Weather forecasts

Although he was a qualified meteorologist, Hopkins ran up a terrible record of forecasting for the TV news programme. He became something of a local joke when a newspaper began keeping a record of his predictions and showed that he'd been wrong almost 300 times in a single year. That kind of notoriety was enough to get him fired. He moved to another part of the country and applied for a similar job. One blank on the job application called for the reason for leaving his previous position. Hopkins wrote, 'The climate didn't agree with me.'

It was autumn, and the Indians on the remote reservation asked their new Chief if the winter was going to be cold or mild. Since he was a new Chief in a modern society, he had never been taught the old secrets, and when he looked at the sky, he couldn't tell what the weather was going to be. Nevertheless, to be on the safe side, he replied to his tribe that the winter was indeed going to be cold and that the members of the village should collect wood to be prepared. But also, being a practical leader, after several days he got an idea. He went to the phone booth, called the National Weather Service and asked, 'Is the coming winter going to be cold?'

'It looks like this winter is going to be quite cold indeed,' the meteorologist at the weather service responded.

So the Chief went back to his people and told them to collect even more wood in order to be prepared. A week later he called the National Weather Service again. 'Is it going to be a very cold winter?'

'Yes,' the man at the National Weather Service again replied, 'it's going to be a very cold winter.'

The Chief again went back to his people and ordered them to collect every scrap of wood they could find. Two weeks later he called the National Weather Service again. 'Are you absolutely sure that the winter is going to be very cold?'

'Absolutely,' the man replied. 'It's going to be one of the coldest winters ever.'

'How can you be so sure?' the Chief asked.

The weatherman replied, 'The Indians are collecting wood like crazy!'

If you are standing in the main street of Amsterdam, and can't see the clock-tower of the Central Railway Station, that means it is raining. If you can see the clock-tower, that means it is about to rain.

An honest weatherman says, 'Today's forecast is bright and sunny with an 80 per cent chance that I'm wrong.'

Who is it that everybody listens to but nobody believes?

The weatherman.

Probably the last completely accurate forecast was when God told Noah there was a 100 per cent chance of precipitation.

A film crew was on location deep in the desert. One day an old Indian went up to the director and said, 'Tomorrow, rain.' The next day it rained.

A week later, the Indian went up to the director and said, 'Tomorrow, storm.' The next day there was a hailstorm.

'This Indian is incredible,' said the director. He told his secretary to hire the Indian to predict the weather. However, after several successful predictions, the old Indian didn't show up for two weeks.

Finally, the director sent for him. 'I have to shoot a big scene tomorrow,' said the director, 'and I'm depending on you. What will the weather be like?'

The Indian shrugged his shoulders. 'Don't know,' he said. 'Radio broke.'

When I was an engineering student, I worked in a scrapyard during a summer vacation. I used to repair construction equipment.

One afternoon, I was taking apart a piling hammer that had some very large bolts holding it together. One of the nuts had corroded onto the bolt; to free it, I started heating the nut with an oxy-acetylene torch.

As I was doing this, one of the dimmest apprentices I have ever known came along. He asked me what I was doing. I patiently explained that if I heated the nut it would grow larger and release its grip on the bolt, so I could then remove it.

'So things get larger when they get hot, do they?' he asked.

Suddenly, an idea flashed into my mind (I know not from where).

'Yes,' I said, 'that's why days are longer in summer and shorter in winter.'

There was a long pause, then his face cleared.

'You know, I always wondered about that,' he said.

Everybody knows about the Fujita Scale which measures the power of tornados. But nobody really knows what all those types of twisters do to cows. So here is the *Moojita Scale*:

- M0 Tornado: Cows in an open field are spun around parallel to the wind flow and become mildly annoyed.
- M1 Tornado: Cows are tipped over and can't get up.
- M2 Tornado: Cows begin rolling with the wind.
- M3 Tornado: Cows tumble and bounce.
- M4 Tornado: Cows are airborne.
- M5 Tornado: *Steak!*

There's a technical term for a sunny, warm day which follows two rainy days. It's called Monday.

Why do forecast models often suffer from depression? They are told they are unattractive and wrong much of the time.

What did the primary rainbow say to the secondary rainbow? Your pants are on backwards.

'You never get anything right,' complained the teacher. 'What kind of job do you think you'll get when you leave school?'

'Well, I want to be the weather girl on TV.'

Q. Why do mother kangaroos hate rainy days?

A. Because then the children have to play inside.

At the height of the gale, the harbourmaster radioed a coastguard on the spot and asked him to estimate the wind speed. He replied that he was sorry, but he didn't have a gauge. However, if it was any help, the wind had just blown his Land Rover off the cliff.

Aberdeen Evening Express

Commenting on a complaint from a Mr Arthur Purdey about a large gas bill, a spokesman for North West gas said, 'We agree it was rather high for the time of year. It's possible Mr Purdey has been charged for the gas used up during the explosion that blew his house to pieces.'

Bangkok Post

Wickedness

God's email

One day God was looking down at earth and saw all of the rascally behaviour that was going on. So he called one of his angels and sent the angel to earth for a time.

When he returned, he told God, 'Yes, it is bad on Earth; 95 per cent are misbehaving and only 5 per cent are not.'

God thought for a moment and said, 'Maybe I had better send down a second angel to get another opinion.'

So God called another angel and sent him to earth for a time too.

When the angel returned he went to God and said, 'Yes, it's true. The earth is in decline; 95 per cent are misbehaving, but 5 per cent are being good.'

God was not pleased. So he decided to email the 5 per cent who were good because he wanted to encourage them, to give them a little something to help them keep going.

Do you know what the email said?

No?

OK, just wondering. I didn't get one either.

Wisdom

- There's always a lot to be thankful for if you take time to look for it. For example, I am sitting here thinking how nice it is that wrinkles don't hurt.
- The easiest way to find something lost around the house is to buy a replacement.
- You don't stop laughing because you grow old. You grow old because you stop laughing.
- The older you get, the tougher it is to lose weight, because by then your body and your fat are really good friends.
- He who hesitates is probably right.
- If you can smile when things go wrong, you have someone in mind to blame.
- The purpose of a child's middle name is so he can tell when he's really in trouble.
- How long a minute is depends on what side of the bathroom door you're on.
- If ignorance is bliss, why aren't a lot more people happy?
- Most of us go to our graves with our music still inside us.
- Don't cry because it's over: smile because it happened.
- We could learn a lot from crayons: some are sharp, some are pretty, some are dull, some have weird names, and all are different colours. But they all have to learn to live in the same box.
- Everything should be made as simple as possible, but no simpler.
- A truly happy person is one who can enjoy the scenery on a detour.
- Happiness sometimes comes through doors you didn't even know you left open.
- Once over the hill, you pick up speed.
- If not for *stress*, some days I'd have no energy at all.
- Whatever hits the fan will not be evenly distributed.
- Everyone has a photographic memory. Some just don't have film.
- Dogs have owners. Cats have staff.
- We cannot change the direction of the wind, but we can adjust our sails.
- If the shoe fits, buy it in every colour.

Work

There is a dangerous virus being passed electronically, orally and by hand. This virus is called *Work*. If you receive Work from any of your colleagues, your boss or anyone else via any means, *do not touch it*. This virus will wipe out your private life completely. If you should come into contact with Work, put your jacket on and take two good friends to the nearest pub.

Purchase the antidote known as Beer. The quickest acting is called *Stella*, but this is only available for those who can afford it. The NHS equivalent is *Carling*. Take the antidote repeatedly until Work has been completely eliminated from your system.

Forward this warning to five friends. If you do not have five friends you have already been infected and Work is controlling your life. This virus is *deadly*.

> One of the symptoms of an approaching nervous breakdown is the belief that one's work is terribly important.
> *Bertrand Russell*

Worms

A minister decided that a visual demonstration would add emphasis to his Sunday sermon.

Four worms were placed into four separate jars. The first worm was put into a container of alcohol. The second worm was put into a container of cigarette smoke. The third worm was put into a container of chocolate syrup. The fourth worm was put into a container of good clean soil.

At the conclusion of the sermon, the minister reported the following results:

- The first worm in alcohol: *Dead.*
- The second worm in cigarette smoke: *Dead.*
- Third worm in chocolate syrup: *Dead.*
- Fourth worm in good clean soil: *Alive!*

So the minister asked the congregation: 'What can you learn from this demonstration?'

A little old woman in the back quickly raised her hand and said, 'As long as you drink, smoke and eat chocolate, you won't have worms!'

Worship

Everyone worships something. It is inevitable. It is in our spiritual DNA. We were designed to worship. We were created to be temples. Some people worship power. Some worship money. Some worship possessions. Some worship themselves. And some worship the true and living God.

Buddy Owens

What has been defined for too long as an hour's exercise on Sunday, packaged by enculturated tradition and preserved in doctrinaire posturing is being redefined, unwrapped, and unsealed today. Worship is being redefined in terms of its form and focus. It isn't that valid traditions must be scorned or discarded but that newness must refill them with meaning.

Jack W. Hayford

It is in the process of being worshipped that God communicates his presence to men.

C. S. Lewis

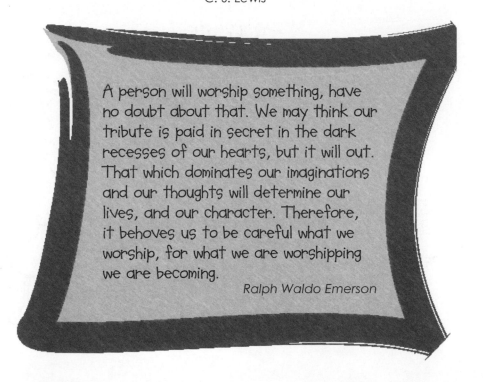

A person will worship something, have no doubt about that. We may think our tribute is paid in secret in the dark recesses of our hearts, but it will out. That which dominates our imaginations and our thoughts will determine our lives, and our character. Therefore, it behoves us to be careful what we worship, for what we are worshipping we are becoming.

Ralph Waldo Emerson

Xmas

Cracker jokes

- Who is never hungry at Christmas? The turkey: it's always stuffed!
- Why are Christmas trees bad at knitting? Because they keep dropping their needles.
- What do vampires post at Christmas? Fang mail!
- Why was Santa's little helper upset? Because he had low elf esteem!
- What do you get if you cross a snowman with a shark? Frostbite!
- Who delivers presents to cats at Christmas? Santa Paws!
- How do you know if a snowman doesn't like you? He gives you the cold shoulder!
- What do you call a donkey with three legs? Wonkey!
- What does Santa do in his garden? Ho, ho, ho-ing!
- What does a snowman wear on his head? An icecap!

That's Ebay for you!

Christmas is weird. What other time of the year do you sit in front of a dead tree and eat sweets out of your socks?

A woman went to the post office to buy stamps for her Christmas cards. She said to the clerk, 'May I have 50 Christmas stamps?'

The clerk asked, 'What denomination?'

The woman replied, 'God help us. Has it come to this? Give me 6 Catholic, 12 Presbyterian, 10 Lutheran and 22 Baptist.'

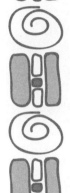

And the Grinch, with his Grinch—feet ice cold in the snow, stood puzzling and puzzling, how could it be so? It came without ribbons. It came without tags. It came without packages, boxes or bags. And he puzzled and puzzled 'till his puzzler was sore. Then the Grinch thought of something he hadn't before. What if Christmas, he thought, doesn't come from a store? What if Christmas, perhaps, means a little bit more?

Dr Seuss, How The Grinch Stole Christmas

So here comes Gabriel again, and what he says is 'Good tidings of great joy...for all people'... That's why the shepherds are first: They represent all the nameless, all the working stiffs, the great wheeling population of the whole world.

Walter Wangerin

Christmas was fast approaching when I reminded my eight—year—old son, Ken, that he would soon be visiting Santa Claus. He seemed unusually resistant to the idea. I asked: 'You do believe in Santa, don't you?'

He thought hard, then said, 'Yes, but I think this is the last year.'

1.9 billion Christmas cards are sent to friends and loved ones every year, making Christmas the largest card-sending occasion in the United States. The second largest is Valentine's Day, with approximately 192 million cards being given.

Hallmark

...Christians buy things. Lots of things. Especially during the Christmas season when we celebrate the birth of the man who said, 'Give up your possessions and follow me.'

David Waters

1 Corinthians chapter 13 (the Christmas version)

If I decorate my house perfectly with plaid bows, strands of twinkling lights and shiny balls, but do not show love to my family, I'm just another decorator.

If I slave away in the kitchen, baking dozens of Christmas delicacies, preparing gourmet meals and arranging a beautifully adorned table at mealtime, but do not show love to my family, I'm just another cook.

If I work at a soup kitchen, sing carols in the nursing home, and give all that I have to charity, but do not show love to my family, it profits me nothing.

If I trim the spruce with shimmering angels and crocheted snowflakes, attend a myriad of holiday parties and sing in the choir's cantata, but do not focus on Christ, I have missed the point.

Love stops the cooking to hug the child. Love sets aside the decorating to kiss the spouse. Love is kind, though harried and tired. Love does not envy another's home that has coordinated Christmas china and table linens. Love does not yell at the kids to get out of the way, but is thankful they are there to be in the way. Love does not give only to those who are able to give in return, but rejoices in giving to those who cannot.

Love bears all things, believes all things, hopes all things, and endures all things. Love never fails.

Video games will break, pearl necklaces will be lost, golf clubs will rust; but giving the gift of love will endure.

As a teacher, Ms Jones, was very curious about how each of her students celebrated Christmas. She called on young Patrick Murphy.

'Tell me, Patrick – what do you do at Christmas time?'

Patrick addressed the class: 'Well, Ms Jones, me and my twelve brothers and sisters go to the midnight Mass and we sing hymns, then we come home very late and we put mince pies by the back door and hang up our stockings. Then, all excited, we go to bed and wait for Father Christmas to come with all our toys.'

'Very nice, Patrick,' she said. 'Now, Jimmy Brown, what do you do at Christmas?'

'Well, Ms Jones, me and my sister also go to Church with Mum and Dad and we sing carols and we get home ever so late. We put cookies and milk by the chimney and we hang up our stockings. We hardly sleep, waiting for Santa Claus to bring our presents.'

Realizing there was a Jewish boy in the class and not wanting to leave him out of the discussion, she asked, 'Now, Isaac Cohen, what do you do at Christmas?'

Isaac said, 'Well, it's the same thing every year. Dad comes home from the office. We all pile into the Rolls Royce, then we drive to his toy factory. When we get inside, we look at all the empty shelves and begin to sing "What a Friend We Have in Jesus". Then we all go to the Bahamas...'

More than 2 million Londoners find Christmas a stressful event, according to research released this week by TalktoaCounsellor.co.uk. They said that 2.3 million Londoners find the celebration causes them high levels of stress.

On that night in Bethlehem, God breathed our air for the first time.
Rich Mullins

His arrival was eagerly anticipated, but not just by children.
He came on Christmas Day, but not down the chimney.
He worked in a wood shop, but not making toys.
He had a beard, but it was not white.
He had some helpers, but they were not elves.
He did a miracle, but not on 34th Street.
He rode into town, but not in a sleigh.
He carried a lot of weight, but he was not heavy.
He hung on a tree, but not as an ornament.
He disappeared into the clouds, but not to the North Pole.
His return is eagerly anticipated, but not predictable.
He is Jesus.
So every year at Christmas time
Let the traditions become a sign
To point us back so long ago
When God came to earth for the world to know.

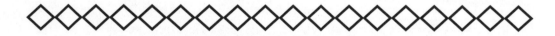

Shopping mall Santas may not have an easy job after all. According to a survey, 90 per cent of all seasonal Santas say that at least one kid pulls their beard every single day – just to see if it is real. The same survey showed that these Santas get sneezed on up to 10 times a day. A third of Santas report being wet on by a child. Nearly three quarters of the kids who sit on Santa's lap say they were 'good' this year, according to the Santas. Yet the survey shows Santa may be getting cynical. These Santas believe that only 50 per cent of the before-mentioned children were actually good during the year.

Source: Reuters

Youth

The young always have the same problem, how to rebel and conform at the same time. They have now solved this by defying their parents and copying one another.

Quentin Crisp

Youth would be an ideal state if it came a little later in life.

Herbert Henry Asquith

The invention of the teenager was a mistake. Once you identify a period of life in which people get to stay out late but don't have to pay taxes – naturally, no one wants to live any other way.

Judith Martin

Youth is the best time to be rich, and the best time to be poor.

Euripides

God...frequently...makes young men and women wiser than the aged, and gives to many, in a very short time, a closer and deeper communion with himself than others attain in a long course of years.

John Wesley

Zeal

Lawn Chair Larry

The following story is my absolute favourite example of *zeal* – of a passion that overrides all reason.

Larry Walters of Los Angeles is one of the few to contend for the Darwin Awards and live to tell the tale. 'I have fulfilled my twenty-year dream,' said Walters, a former truck driver for a company that makes TV commercials. 'I'm staying on the ground. I've proved the thing works.'

Larry's boyhood dream was to fly. But fates conspired to keep him from his dream. He joined the Air Force, but his poor eyesight disqualified him from the job of pilot. After he was discharged from the military, he sat in his backyard watching jets fly overhead.

He hatched his weather balloon scheme while sitting outside in his 'extremely comfortable' Sears lawnchair. He purchased 45 weather balloons from an Army–Navy surplus store, tied them to his tethered lawnchair dubbed the *Inspiration I*, and filled the 4-foot-diameter balloons with helium. Then he strapped himself into his lawnchair with some sandwiches, Miller Lite, and a pellet gun. He figured he would pop a few of the many balloons when it was time to descend.

Larry's plan was to sever the anchor and lazily float up to a height of about 30 feet above his back yard, where he would enjoy a few hours of flight before coming back down. But things didn't work out quite as Larry planned.

When his friends cut the cord anchoring the lawnchair to his Jeep, he did not float lazily up to 30 feet. Instead, he streaked into the LA sky as if shot from a cannon, pulled by the lift of 42 helium balloons holding 33 cubic feet of helium each. He didn't level off at 100 feet, nor did he level off at 1,000 feet. After climbing and climbing, he levelled off at 16,000 feet.

At that height he felt he couldn't risk shooting any of the balloons, lest he unbalance the load and really find himself in trouble. So he stayed there, drifting, cold and frightened, with his beer and sandwiches, for more than 14 hours. He crossed the primary approach corridor of LAX, where TransWorld Airlines and Delta Airlines pilots radioed in reports of the strange sight.

Eventually he gathered the nerve to shoot a few balloons, and slowly descended. The hanging tethers tangled and caught in a power line, blacking out a Long Beach neighbourhood for 20 minutes. Larry climbed to safety, where he was arrested by waiting members of the LAPD. As he was led away in handcuffs, a reporter dispatched to cover the daring rescue asked him why he had done it. Larry replied nonchalantly, 'A man can't just sit around.'

The Federal Aviation Administration was not amused. Safety Inspector Neal Savoy said, 'We know he broke some part of the Federal Aviation Act, and as soon as we decide which part it is, a charge will be filed.'

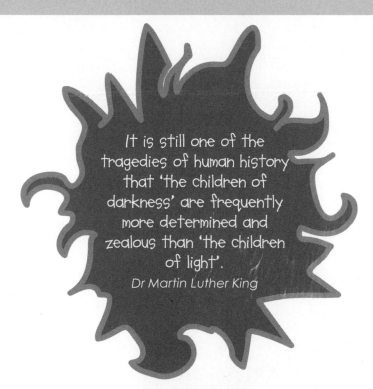

It is still one of the tragedies of human history that 'the children of darkness' are frequently more determined and zealous than 'the children of light'.

Dr Martin Luther King

Zen

Q. What did the Zen Buddhist say to the hot dog vendor?

A. 'Make me one with everything.'

On presenting a £5 note to the vendor, he asked for his change. The vendor replied, 'But change comes from within.'